D.BLK ST

Something Must Be Done

Peggy Wood. Photograph by Rayburn Beale; courtesy of the artist.

Something Must Be Done

One Black Woman's Story

Peggy Wood

with Parker Brown

With a Foreword by H. Douglas Barclay

SYRACUSE UNIVERSITY PRESS

First Edition 2006
06   07   08   09   10   11   6   5   4   3   2   1

The authors wish to thank photographer Rayburn Beale for his kind help
in the early stages of this project.

The paper used in this publication meets the minimum requirements of American
National Standard for Information Sciences—Permanence of Paper for Printed
Library Materials, ANSI Z39.48–1984.∞™

Library of Congress Cataloging-in-Publication Data

Wood, Peggy, 1912–
Something must be done : one Black woman's story / Peggy Wood with Parker
Brown ; with a foreword by H. Douglas Barclay.—1st ed.
p. cm.
ISBN 0–8156–0877–2 (hardcover : alk. paper)
1. Wood, Peggy, 1912– 2. African American women civil rights workers—
Biography. 3. Civil rights workers—United States—Biography. 4. African
American women—Biography. 5. African Americans—Civil rights—New York
(State)—Syracuse—History—20th century. 6. Syracuse (N.Y.)—Biography. 7.
Poughkeepsie (N.Y.)—Biography. 8. Lima (Ohio)—Biography. 9. Middle class—
Southern States—Biography. 10. Southern States—Race relations—History—20th
century. I. Brown, Parker. II. Title.
E185.97.W76A3 2006
323.092—dc22
[B]   2006017823

Manufactured in the United States of America

In memory of Frank Tucker Wood, Jr.

I maintain that I have been a Negro three times—a Negro baby, a Negro girl and a Negro woman. Still, if you have received no clear cut impression of what the Negro in America is like, then you are in the same place with me. There is no *The Negro* here. Our lives are so diversified, internal attitudes so varied, appearances and capabilities so different, that there is no possible classification so catholic that it will cover us all, except My people! My people!

—Zora Neale Hurston, *Dust Tracks on a Road*

Peggy Wood, a former social worker, witnessed nearly a century of black advancement and participated in the struggle to achieve it. Hers is a story of the segregated South before World War II, the black community center movement in the North in the 1940s, and the campaign for civil rights in Syracuse, New York, in the 1950s and 1960s.

Parker Brown, a tax attorney by day, is an oral historian committed to capturing important stories that fell below the radar of the mainstream media in years gone by. His particular interest is in the social history behind headline-making developments.

Contents

Illustrations

Donors

In honor of Peggy Wood

Doug and DeeDee Barclay

The Central New York Community Foundation, Inc.
in recognition of Peggy's service
on the CNYCF board

Foreword

Many of us would like to think that we "made a difference" during our years in public life. Peggy Wood is a person who unquestionably did.

I have known Peggy for at least thirty years as a bright, dynamic, and dignified woman who took on one community issue after another in Syracuse, New York, addressing problems and solving them with quiet persistence. That in itself would warrant the publication of her memoir. But these recollections give the reader so much more.

Peggy's life has been an extraordinary journey through the history of our country. In *Something Must Be Done,* we have a splendid chronicle of middle-class black family life as well as a panoramic view of both the South and the North in the twentieth century. We see the strategies used by a highly educated family for coping with segregation, and the family's constant assertion that all people are created equal. As the decades go by and the civil rights struggle of the 1950s and 1960s recedes into the past, it is well to be reminded of the bad old days for so many Americans— and of the people like Peggy Wood who were not willing to accept injustice.

This memoir is in many ways a social history, illuminating

what happened behind the scenes, conveying how it felt to sit in the back of the bus. It is also the story of a remarkable woman who helped change her community for the better.

How pleased I am that all of this has been recorded for future generations.

H. Douglas Barclay
United States Ambassador to El Salvador
San Salvador, El Salvador

Preface

Three years ago I asked the advice of Walter Welsh, former rector of Grace Episcopal Church in Syracuse, New York. Father Welsh had been a leading participant in the drive to desegregate Syracuse back in the 1950s and 1960s. I explained to him that I hoped to carry my tape recorder here and there—like Studs Terkel, to be honest about it—interviewing people and capturing some of the social history of our city. A native of Virginia myself, I was particularly interested, I told him, in the recollections of people who had left the South and moved to the North. In Syracuse, that meant primarily black people.

When I asked Walter whom he would suggest I interview, he thought for a moment. Then he said, "She is not exactly what you have in mind, but I would suggest you start with Peggy Wood."

I was slightly acquainted with Peggy Wood—Mrs. Frank T. Wood, Jr.—from evening prayer on Wednesday nights at Grace Church. Although nearly ninety years old at the time, she would drive herself to church each week. Peggy had, it was clear, a go-ahead attitude. Concessions to age were not in her playbook. But from a distance I didn't know much more. She was gracious, dignified, and warm, I would have said—and rightly—but perhaps not conventionally "sweet" or grandmotherly. Something intangible suggested that this was a person to be reckoned with.

When I outlined the project to Peggy, she was understandably perplexed. What *can* this man be talking about? Her experiences did not consist simply of living in the South and moving to the North. Far from it, as I was about to learn. But she kindly agreed to let me tape her recollections in what I imagine was a "Hail Mary" spirit. If we try this, something, on the off chance, might come of it.

Peggy said, "It's so hard for people outside of the black community to see any blacks other than those who have been lifted up and brought on." Early in our taping sessions it became obvious that she herself had not been lifted up and brought on. It was also obvious that the primary reason for this was education. W. E. B. Du Bois wrote of education as a "pillar of fire by night" guiding an oppressed people. Peggy's family had followed this pillar from the days after the Civil War. Du Bois could have been describing Peggy's father when he wrote, "I sit with Shakespeare and he winces not. Across the color line I move arm in arm with Balzac and Dumas, where smiling men and welcoming women glide in gilded hall."[1]

Peggy's point was not that more should be known about the black elite, but that black experience, like white experience, comes in many forms. As Zora Neale Hurston memorably asserts in a passage forming the epigraph to this book, "there is no *The Negro* here." The same outsiders who could see black people only as "lifted up" also tended to see black people as all of one kind. This was an attitude, I soon discovered, that Peggy was intent upon rebutting with the story of her own experience.

---

1. W. E. Burghardt Du Bois, *The Souls of Black Folk* (1903; reprint, New York: Vintage Books/Library of America, 1990), 11.

And what experience it was, spanning most of the twentieth century. When Peggy was a child, primarily in the South, there stood, in Du Bois's words, "two separate worlds; and separate not simply in the higher realms of social intercourse, but also in church and school, on railway and streetcar, in hotels and theatres, in streets and city sections, in books and newspapers, in asylums and jails, in hospitals and graveyards."[2] The early part of Peggy's story describes a black person's navigation through the rocks and shoals of this segregated society, including a brush with the Ku Klux Klan. But, in another sense, it is the story of seceding from the white world into black enclaves of culture and attainment. Both the many black college campuses where Peggy lived with her academic parents and the Auburn Avenue section of black Atlanta can be seen this way. For many readers, this window into early-twentieth-century middle-class black folkways will be a revelation.

But Peggy's story, early and late, is also about Peggy as a person, regardless of her color. We see her growing to maturity in a household where the expectations for the children were high indeed. We see her flourishing, but, at the same time, perhaps a little weary. The circumstances of Peggy Wright's marriage in 1937 to Frank Wood—a touching story not to be revealed prematurely—may be seen as a declaration of independence from some of these family expectations.

During the 1940s, we follow Peggy, now a graduate of the School of Social Work in Atlanta, as she and Frank move to Lima, Ohio, to start their own family, and later to Poughkeepsie, New York. These are the years when Peggy became involved with black community centers, vital institutions for people who were gener-

2. W. E. Burghardt Du Bois, quoted in E. Franklin Frazier, *Black Bourgeoisie* (1957; reprint, New York: Free Press Paperbacks, 1997), 148.

ally excluded from white social services. In Lima she receives a valuable lesson in humility. In Poughkeepsie her tendency to "stir things up" comes into view, as well as her practical reforming spirit. In our taping sessions, Peggy recalled herself thinking, "something must be done" about schools that excluded black children or social service agencies that ignored the black community.

Writing in 1940 in *An American Dilemma,* Gunnar Myrdal clearly describes the situation Peggy was facing in the North. At that time, many institutions—schools, parks, playgrounds, stores, and theaters, for example—had a community basis; residential segregation was, therefore, an effective means of keeping black people apart from white. School boundaries, to take only one example, were usually set at the line between white and black neighborhoods. Residential segregation thus created segregation in other aspects of life, even in hospitals, clinics, relief agencies, and other institutions.

But by the forties, Peggy notes, "things were beginning to boil up from down under in the black community. Changes were about to be made, and everybody sensed it." Returning soldiers formed one catalyst for these changes; black soldiers who had served their country in World War II came home expecting decent treatment in civilian life.

By 1950, Peggy's story shifts to Syracuse, New York, where Frank Wood took a job as director of the community center. Here begins Peggy's public career, as a social worker first for the Salvation Army until 1958 and then for the city health department. In her first role, we can observe her working for the betterment of her clients, black and white. But she also sees that "something must be done" about the exclusion of black teenagers from maternity homes—and she does it. Her recollections of these Salvation Army years reveal not only her practical, problem-solving bent, but also her nonjudgmental nature. On tape she spoke affectionately about her clients, a tone that cannot always be translated to the printed page.

Peggy's recollections of her health department years give us a personal perspective on how Syracuse worked in the late 1950s and early to mid-1960s, where this account ends. We watch as urban renewal transforms—*devastates* is another word—Syracuse's heavily black Fifteenth Ward. We witness the creation of Syracuse's Commission on Human Rights, as well as the establishment of a highly innovative program for pregnant teenagers called YMED.

Most descriptions of the civil and human rights struggle, in Syracuse as elsewhere, focus on demonstrations in the street. Peggy's story is not a counternarrative but a companion narrative. Here we see gains made, largely behind the scenes, by a "specimen," as she calls herself, of that rare breed: the black, female insider. One of the impulses of this publication is to lay that narrative beside the more familiar one in order to give a richer picture of a turbulent time.

As Peggy's absorbing story spooled onto the tape recorder, my original plan of interviewing numerous people became a plan to interview Peggy and two or three others. Finally, as the richness of her account became clear, this gave way to a decision to interview only Peggy. Less, in this instance, is more.

Parker Brown

PART ONE

Education, Education, and Education

✿

Childhood on Campus

My father, John Clarence Wright, was born near Charlottesville, Virginia, in 1881, the son of a black man and a Native American woman. The little place where the family lived south of Charlottesville was called Glendower, Virginia—so small it's not even on the map. This was the location of a school established by the Freedmen's Bureau after the Civil War. While I have no proof, I like to think that this school just might have set the Wrights on the path to higher education that they were to follow.

Clarence, my father, was the first child. Soon after his birth, the family moved to Newark, New Jersey, where my grandfather opened a catering business. My grandfather did well, and each of his four children (my father, then two sisters and a brother) became college graduates. Education really was what determined who rose to the top in those years. The Wrights were a family set aside because, with the money from the catering business, the children were able to go to school instead of dropping out to work.

In 1902, after finishing at the public high school in Newark, my father entered a white college, Oberlin, in Ohio, which was almost unheard of in those times. He was one of six black seniors to be graduated from Oberlin in 1906. Back then he was one of six "colored" students. At Oberlin he took part in everything. His is

3

the only black face in a picture I have of his Oberlin fraternity. Dad also seems to have been a student orator. One night in 1904 he delivered a speech titled "Does the American Negro Deserve His Citizenship?" You can bet the answer was yes!

My mother, Addie Streator Wright, born in 1879, was the fourth child of a couple from Shelbyville, Tennessee, about fifty miles below Nashville. My mother's mother, Frances, was the daughter of the owner of a large store in Shelbyville, a man named Stone. He was white and owned slaves. On his plantation, there was a young man, Walter Streator, a very light-skinned slave, who apparently was a capable person. Family tradition has it that Stone gave Streator the run of the place and made him the supervisor of the other slaves. Walter was handsome, and my grandmother Frances fell in love with him at age sixteen.

Stone agreed that his daughter could marry Walter Streator—which leads me to think that Walter must have been so light that he could easily have passed for white. Stone's one condition was that they obtain a proper marriage license from a county in Tennessee. Of course, it was against the law to be married across racial lines. It was a wonder Walter wasn't lynched on the spot. It has come down in the family that Frances and Walter went to sixteen different counties until they finally found a clerk who would grant them a license. In other words, a clerk who was willing to take a chance in an iffy situation. Whether this has gotten better in the retelling, I don't know. But I do know that somehow Frances and Walter got married. Stone built them a house on his property, just as he did for his other daughters.

Walter and Frances had their four children, my mother Addie the last of them in 1879. The family after a time moved from Shelbyville up to Nashville. They went there because of Fisk University. My grandmother wanted her children to graduate from Fisk. She had chosen for her children to grow up as black. This was not an easy thing for her because there was a difference in how her four children looked. Half of them could pass for white; the others could not. A light-skinned person in that day was looked at as different from the other black people. That's what helped you to move up in life—your ability to pass for white. But my mother Addie went to Fisk, a black college, and graduated in 1904.

Fisk was supported in the early days following the Civil War by the American Missionary Association, an arm of the Congregational Church. W. E. B. Du Bois, the great social critic and editor of *The Crisis* for the NAACP, was a graduate. Du Bois's philosophical adversary Booker T. Washington served on Fisk's board of trustees. The American Missionary Association—Aunt Mary Ann, as we called it—and the Du Bois-Washington debate are part of the background to the story of my own early years. More to come on these subjects.

After graduation from Oberlin, my father took a job as an English teacher at a tiny black institution in Lawrenceville in Southside Virginia, St. Paul's Normal and Industrial School. St. Paul's, now a college, was affiliated with the Episcopal Church. It was typical of the large number of small black schools dotted all over the rural south. How microscopic Lawrenceville suited Dad, who grew up near New York City, I do not know. But two years later he moved on to a very different type of school, Tuskegee Institute in Alabama.

Booker T. Washington, the principal of Tuskegee Institute when Dad went there in 1908, was the most famous black man in America at the time. Washington had gone to Tuskegee from Hampton Institute in Virginia in 1881. In the intervening years, he

*Peggy Wood's mother, Addie Streator, left, and her Fisk college
roommate, ca. 1904; courtesy of the author.*

had built Tuskegee up with the help of Northern philanthropy into a large, well-endowed school with many fine buildings and a large faculty. It was far removed from the struggling normal school at a dusty crossroads, which was more typical of the impoverished countryside across the South.

When Dad arrived at Tuskegee, my mother was already there, having come from Fisk. Booker Washington traveled all over the United States, and abroad for that matter, delivering speeches and raising money. He was not much of a scholar, and my mother's major role was to help him write these speeches. Washington was not critical. Mom could add or subtract pretty much as she pleased. She lived in the Oaks, where the Washington family lived. She also taught English.

My father headed the division of English at Tuskegee and taught drama as well. Clarence Wright and Addie Streator crossed paths in the English Department. They fell in love and promptly got married, in Nashville, in 1908.

Dad was not in favor of my mother's working so much for Booker Washington. Dad felt that my mother should have more time for her career, which was teaching. Whether there was any coolness between Booker Washington and my Dad, I do not know. But one surviving letter, dated 1910, doesn't sound very warm:

Mr. Wright:

I am very glad to have had the opportunity of reading the essays which you have sent to me. On the whole I think they are good and they show improvement in the method of teaching. The only adverse criticism that I venture is this: There are too many big words in some of them. The sentences are too long and involved. Nothing is stronger in the teaching of English than to teach the students to use the smallest words possible, and the shortest and most simple sentences. Let them use the same kind of language in writing that they do in talking. For example, I find this sentence in one of the compositions: "The pressed steel wheel has arrived and at the psychological moment when the users of timber have begun to realize that the products of forests have been wastefully misused and that they are face to face with an irreparable timber shortage." I know of no student who uses this kind of language in general conversation. There are other sentences running through the compositions that are equally faulty in this direction.

Booker T. Washington[1]

For whatever reason, later in 1910 my parents were on the move, this time to what was then called Florida Agricultural and Mechanical College for Negroes in Tallahassee.

Unlike all the other schools I grew up in, Florida A&M was state supported, not that this meant a lot of support. Despite its name, A&M was really a normal school in 1910, not yet permitted to grant college degrees. About three hundred students attended, half in what was called the Preparatory Division and half in the Normal Division. Dad headed the English Department and served as dean. My mother was to be in the English Department, but she started her family just then.

My older brother, John Clarence Wright, Jr., was born in 1911. I followed on December 16, 1912. Then came my younger brother, Herbert Hornell Wright, in 1915. In 1918, when we had moved

1. Louis R. Harlan and Raymond W. Smock, eds., *The Booker T. Washington Papers* (Urbana: Univ. of Illinois Press, 1980), 10:311.

away from A&M, my sister Yvonne Marguerite Wright completed the family.

My father named me Martha. He wrote that on the certificate. But my mother did not like the name. When the two of them were having an argument over it, someone apparently suggested that I be named after Peggy, the family puppy. The story goes that my mother thought that this was the best way to stop the argument and agreed to "Peggy." So my father went down to the county courthouse and changed the name to Peggy. For a middle name they selected "Addilee," a variation of Addie Lee, Mom's name.

On the campus in Tallahassee, my brothers and I were insulated. We had no firsthand experience of the evil out in the world. We were as free as anything could be. We could roam all over our little universe without any hesitancy, without any problems, because the entire faculty—both black and white—looked out for us children. But the minute we crossed the line beyond the campus, death was possible. So we also had, as a part of our early education, a sense that we had to be careful.

Anyone who knew the Wright children knew that I called the tune. My mother and father made no bones about it—I was in charge when it came to the younger set. My first realization of this must have been early one morning in Tallahassee. There was a loud yelling out in the front of our house at A&M: "FIRE, FIRE!" My father and mother ran into our rooms. We were to get up—the house was on fire. Get outside and stay there in one spot. So we ran out of the house. There was nothing much that we wanted to take with us. We didn't have toys. We didn't need them. Whatever you did, you did in a group or used whatever was around. But my mother's wedding presents and all sorts of keepsakes went up in this fire.

Peggy and her brothers, John (center) and Herbert; courtesy of the author.

My brothers and I were in our night clothes. We were standing together out of the way, not in any fright. My father came over, and he said, "Peggy, don't you let your brothers run back into the house." I thought, "What would they run back into the house for?" There's nothing there that we would think of as something we needed to save. Dad explained to me what this fire meant to my mother, who had gone to pieces. She wanted to go back in the house and get her wedding presents especially, but the firemen would not permit it.

My father spoke to me as the responsible person, not to my older brother. I felt bigger than a fireman, and that's why I remember it to this day. But that's the way that my father treated me, all through my schooling and right up to the last.

While we were at Florida A&M, the Great War began in Europe. When the United States entered the conflict, the YMCA recruited my father to go to France to help administer its literacy program. Officially, Dad's title was "Y.M.C.A. Secretary and Supervisor of Instruction of Colored Troops with the Army Educational Corps (Overseas)." The YMCA's literacy program was a breeding ground for future leaders of the black community in the United States. John Hope, for instance, later president of the new Atlanta University, served in France with my father.

Black soldiers in the American Expeditionary Forces were segregated from the white soldiers. Many of the black soldiers (and many of the white ones as well) could neither read nor write. The army thought it was imperative that it teach the black troops these skills. I think the reason was that, in their supposed ignorance, the black enlisted men could not get along with the white ones. Or at least the army feared that.

Dad's YMCA papers—"Name: Wright, John C. (colored)"—

place him at "St. Nazaire, University, Beaume, Cote d'Or, South-western Dept." and describe him as, among other things, a "Hut Secretary."[2] The huts were the little makeshift schoolrooms where reading and writing were taught. Dad said the Y had a terrible time trying to get the recruits to admit their illiteracy because they were embarrassed. They could not be persuaded to come into a hut.

As an experiment, my father asked the army to build a boxing ring right next to a hut. The soldiers would go to the ring, they would fight, and then they would be invited into the hut. The soldiers thought they were going in to rest after the boxing match. But in the hut the Y officials told them that the Y hoped to publish the results of the boxing in the camp newspaper. But there would be no point in reporting on the boxing if the participants couldn't read the story. The soldiers were stunned. Dad would tell us that's the way they got some of the first soldiers to cooperate. After this group stuck with the program and liked it, others followed. My father even put on plays for the black troops to draw them into the literacy program.

When my Dad shipped out for France in 1918, the rest of us left Florida A&M and moved to West Medford, Massachusetts, a suburb of Boston. We were taken in by my mother's roommate from Fisk University, a gorgeous black woman passing for white, who was married to a white man. "Passing" meant nothing to us kids. To grown-ups, it did. There were a lot of black people who passed and never came back to the black race again. Some lived forever in fear. Some wouldn't have children and were afraid of being discovered at work.

2. Kautz Family YMCA Archives, Andersen Library, University of Minnesota, Minneapolis, Minnesota.

I think my mother could have passed for white. The roommate probably would never have said "come on and stay with me" if we had been dark. We children were brown skinned, more Indian-looking than anything else. (Everyone called my older brother "Injun" because of his looks.) One of my mother's uncles lived in Chicago and married a black woman who passed for white. She had a job as an usher in a theater. Very white. Beautiful. All of their children could easily have passed for white. But this family officially stayed black. Each of the children married loved ones who were obviously black.

I was five years old when we moved to West Medford. My older brother and I were enrolled in the local grammar school, and my younger brother would soon enter kindergarten. This was my first experience of racial hatred. The folks in West Medford had seldom seen any black people, and they weren't open to new experiences.

My brother John played hooky a lot of the time we were in West Medford. And my brother Herb was too young to notice much. But I felt the hatred when I walked to and from school. People on the way threw objects at me and called me names. I did not react to them, call them names, or curse them out. I walked through it as though it wasn't happening. Then I got to the school and met the same situation with the children.

The whole time I was in West Medford, I suffered violent headaches. As I look back, I think they were all made up. I'm sure my mother had the doctor check me. And probably with the kind of headaches that I claimed, I would have been dead before we ever got out of West Medford! My mother accepted my statement that I had a headache and did not send me to school. No one at the school cared when John played hooky or when I spent day after day at home supposedly ill. So I managed to get through what turned out to be two years in West Medford on my sickbed.

My father came back from France to the United States and West Medford for a visit during the war. His visit must have coincided with Armistice Day, November 11, 1918, because I remember his taking us to a huge parade in Boston celebrating the war's end. Dad was so proud because of what he was doing in Europe. As presents he brought big, beautiful straw hats—one for my mother and one for me. For the boys he brought garrison caps. Dad took the family, I remember, to a bridge over a river. But as soon as we got to this bridge, John and I threw our hats in the water. That gesture stayed with my father for as long as he lived. The reason we threw our hats in the river was that it was horrible for us to live in West Medford. When my dad came back so joyous about France and bringing these lovely hats, our only method of showing the way we felt was to throw those hats in the water. It was spontaneous. I don't think he recognized that John and I were hiding out in West Medford the way you do when you are trying to avoid jail.

I don't think my mother fully realized the situation either. She had her college roommate whose company she enjoyed. Mom liked the piano. We kids would stand around it singing while she played the war songs. She would stop and say, "The next time Dad comes home and he brings something for you, don't you dare. . . !"

By 1919 when my father came home for good, my little sister, Yvonne Marguerite, had been born. She was named after a nurse attached to the literacy program in France. The reason Dad gave was that this nurse had done such good work for the black soldiers. Mom was apparently content to commemorate this saintly nurse!

Now it was time to leave West Medford. The YMCA offered my father a position with the New York City Y, the one for black people on 135th Street, which was to play a role in the Harlem Renaissance of the 1920s. We moved to New York and lived in Brooklyn with my mother's sister Daphne.

Aunt Daphne had one child, who was grown and serving in the Navy. This was considered a very good job by blacks and carried a lot of prestige. Her husband was a Pullman porter, another prestigious job in the black community. The mailmen and the Pullman porters were at the top of the heap. He worked on the train that went from Washington to Boston and catered to politicians and wealthy folks. Aunt Daphne and her husband could afford to own their own home, a three-story brownstone. The neighborhood was an exclusive one for blacks at that time. It was the old upper-crust area before the rise of Harlem.

Our family had the third floor of Aunt Daphne's house. The windows from the living room looked out on the sidewalk. My brothers and I would peer out, but we were afraid to go outside at first until the neighborhood children accepted us—which they soon did. The local elementary school was close enough for us to walk. My little brother, who was two grades under me, and I usually went together, holding hands. There was none of the hostility of West Medford because there were no white people around. In 1919, ugly race riots broke out all over the United States, but we came and went without fear in this totally black world.

I liked Brooklyn, but this was just a temporary move. My father had made it clear to the Y that he wanted to go back to teaching in a black college in the South. I remember that adults there in Brooklyn were always talking about the horrors for blacks in the Jim Crow South. They had come out of it, they had made it, and things were working out fine for them. They wouldn't go back down South for the *world.*

My father was soon being courted by Edward Waters College, a small black institution on the outskirts of Jacksonville, Florida, affiliated with the African Methodist Episcopal Church. I was seven or eight years old at the time. My brothers and I were invited to a meeting at the 135th Street Y. Officials of the college were present, as well as the white philanthropists from the North who made schools like Edward Waters possible. To appeal to us children, these adults said that they would provide our family a parlor car on the train to Jacksonville. But they told us that we could not lift the shades, that we would have to go from New York to Jacksonville with the shades down. It wouldn't do for any little black faces to appear at the window of a fancy car like that!

Dad accepted the presidency of Edward Waters College, and we got the parlor car. It was like two or three rooms put together. We kept the shades down as we were told, but every now and then my brothers and I peeped out when no white folks were around. To us it was all one great adventure.

Edward Waters had two large dormitories. The one for boys, where we lived, was down the road quite a ways from the main campus with the girls' dorm, the administration building, the classroom buildings, and the school for faculty children. Although I didn't realize this at the time, the president's quarters were at one end of the boys' dorm for a reason. If the Ku Klux Klan came after the president, the male students and the male teachers who also lived in the building could hear the warning bell and come out— guns and all. A barbed wire fence taller than a six-foot person circled the dorm. There was a road in the front and a field in the back. At ten o'clock taps, the front gates were locked and a guard came on duty.

When we first arrived, college officials introduced us to the trunk room near our quarters. Each one of us children was given a trunk. When the alarm sounded, we were to go to our trunk, get in that trunk, and pull the lid down until whatever happened was over. An attack by the Klan especially. Mine was an old-fashioned truck about three feet high and two feet wide and three or four feet long. High on the wall of the trunk room was a little window similar to a transom. We could stand on a trunk and look out to see what was going on outside.

The barbed wire and the guards and the trunks for hiding caused me to be fearful, but this was mixed with many carefree times, as happens with children. I liked peeping out the transom. I liked the big sleeping porch attached to our quarters. I also liked the little world we children had inside the barbed wire fence.

The groundskeeper, who also managed the college farm and gardens, provided all kinds of activities for us. He would bring the horses out for us to ride, both with a saddle and without. But bottle wars were my favorite. I much preferred this to playing with dolls!

There were two kinds of bottles, green and clear, which the groundskeeper would collect for us. They represented opposing armies. You were on one side or the other, the green or the clear. A bottle had to have a neck on it like a Coca-Cola bottle so that you could tie a string around it. You'd have all the green soldiers on this side and all the clear soldiers on that side. You would drag those things around. You would hide and, all of a sudden, you'd make some noise and out would come yours and out would come theirs. You would fight with the bottles to see whose bottle got broken first. The groundskeeper would talk about real wars that had been fought. He would say, "Now in the history book, you had such and such a thing." Lord help me, we made such a fuss.

We used to go to the movies on Saturday in Jacksonville. I thought this was a wonderful day because they had serials. You'd see one, and it would be continued the next Saturday, all silent, of course. We sat in the Jim Crow seats in the balcony. The steps to it were not even inside the theater itself. My parents broke down and let us go to this theater. Some other faculty parents did not let their children attend.

The parents whose children were not allowed to go were critical of the parents whose children went. There was quite a discussion when they all got together because that was really letting down the race to go to one of those segregated theaters. We had all the protection that was necessary. It was just the thought of giving your money to the white people who would segregate. But every place that we would live, including Atlanta, had segregated theaters. In Atlanta you had the Fox Theater, where Negroes had to sit in the balcony. They had these steps that went up on the outside of this building.

At the theaters where we went to see the Saturday serials, I don't think they ever had any black films. But black movies were shown on the Edward Waters campus, I'm sure. I can definitely remember them later on when we had moved to other colleges, particularly movies with Paul Robeson.

To the side of the boys' dormitory, there was a grocery run by a white family named Parramore. The Parramores lived behind the store. They had children my age who crawled under the fence and played bottle games with us. We were friendly with Mr. Parramore and with his children. When my parents went away, which they did all the time, they would ask Mr. Parramore to keep an eye on us kids.

After the First World War, the Ku Klux Klan came back to life all over the United States and especially in Florida. There was viciousness all the time. The rumor went around that the president of Edward Waters was targeted. If he drove to town—in a big Packard at the time—he was supposed to be shot. My father kept going to town and nothing happened. Others were not so fortunate. Two male teachers were assaulted in the night, slashed with knives, and had salt poured into their wounds. Naturally no arrests were made.

But worse was to come. A young black man who sold ice cream from a cart to us kids had his head cut off and placed on the porch of the girls' dormitory. Everyone was terrified. My father and mother decided they had had enough of Jacksonville. Dad decided that he would resign as president of Edward Waters. There was no way to get the white community to do anything about the atrocities. The truth is that most white people didn't want Edward Waters there anyway: "As soon as you get them out of here, the better."

After the murder of the ice cream vendor, my father went over to talk to Mr. Parramore. Dad had been tipped off by somebody in town that Parramore was head of the Ku Klux Klan. Parramore denied it. But when my father came out of Parramore's store, he was sure that the tip was true. Parramore knew so much about the threats made against the teachers that my father's suspicions were confirmed. Later I believe Parramore admitted to my father that he was the head. Parramore promised that the outrages would stop, but Dad didn't believe him.

Before we left, the Ku Klux Klan marched by the campus in full uniform. Dad would have loved to have had a cannon and killed every single one—just stood there and ripped them right down, including Parramore. I think that was his feeling. He did not grow up in the South. My mother did, and she was less surprised. The Klan activity was such a blow to my dad that he could not have stayed there under any circumstances.

From Jacksonville we moved, in 1924, to Daytona, Florida, where Dad accepted the vice presidency of what was then called Daytona-Cookman Collegiate Institute, now Bethune-Cookman College. The president was Mary McLeod Bethune, the famous black educator who would later advise Franklin Roosevelt. Mrs. Bethune wanted to have Dad as her vice president because she was traveling all over the United States as *the* person who knew black colleges and the problems that black people had. Dad sometimes traveled with her, but more often he minded the store while she was away. She was a very strong, very opinionated woman, but my father seemed to get along with her. My mother didn't do quite as well!

Daytona-Cookman had been founded by Mary McLeod Bethune as the Daytona Educational and Industrial Training School for Negro Girls. Just before we arrived, it had become coeducational by merger with Cookman Institute. It was in the process of affiliating with the Methodist Church. Daytona-Cookman, like many of the other little black "colleges" in the South, was really a high school at the time but adding college-level instruction as rapidly as possible.

Ours was not the type of black family that white folks normally imagined. In Daytona, the college built a big, two-story house for us, which my father designed. It was stucco, beige trimmed with green, with four bedrooms upstairs. It had a lovely porch across the back and a library with lots of windows. Next to the library was a sitting room with a fireplace and windows facing the street. Dad put on many Shakespearean plays throughout the years he was with various colleges. The student actors would always be coming to our house, as well as the choirs that sang spirituals. These young people would congregate at Daytona-Cookman in that sitting room. As a family, we would discuss plays. My mother would read Chaucer to us.

Someone came in to do the cooking, and a chauffeur was on call to drive our big Chandler. Actually, we had two cars at Daytona. Someone sold my father a used red convertible, an English roadster and as sporty as anything. Dad just had a fit over it. He drove that car himself. It had a rumble seat in the back. That's where two of us kids sat. My mother and father and the two who were least likely to get along with the rest of us sat up front.

Both my father and mother were actively involved with the Black Parent-Teachers Association for Florida. My mother was a paid executive. Our trips as a family were mostly to Jacksonville because that's where the headquarters of the Parent-Teachers Association for Florida was located. It seems to me as I look back that we drove—in the Chandler—through something like a jungle to get to Jacksonville. Jacksonville had more social life for black adults than Daytona did. But there were not that many black people in Daytona, other than those associated with the college, who had enough funds to go *anywhere.*

My father would also drive me in the roadster over to what we called "the water." That's where the wealthy benefactors of Daytona-Cookman lived in the winter, facing the ocean. He would visit them on behalf of the college. To get there, you had to drive across a causeway. Black people could not cross that causeway unless they were invited or unless they worked for one of the wealthy white families. You had to have a pass. People at the college wouldn't even have thought about trying to get to the beach to go

Family in front of the Wrights' house, Daytona Beach, Florida, at what came to be called Bethune-Cookman College, ca. 1925. Back row, left to right: Peggy's grandmother Frances Streator, Peggy's father Clarence, and a cousin; front row, left to right: John, Yvonne, Herbert, and Peggy Wright; courtesy of the author.

swimming. It's a miracle when you find blacks two generations back who grew up in the South who knew how to swim because it was so difficult for them to get to the water. But, both at Jacksonville and Daytona, there were out-of-the-way places where blacks could swim. I remember because my dad swore by salt water as a cure every time I got a boil.

My father and Mrs. Bethune drove together up the East Coast from time to time to New York City to visit the General Education Board founded by John D. Rockefeller. There were certain communities where the black churches would have their kitchens open so black people traveling through could stop for a meal. But there weren't enough churches doing this, and blacks had to try their luck sometimes in restaurants. Dad loved to tell the story about some little town in South Carolina where he and Mrs. Bethune stopped at a diner. They went in the door, and the counter man said, "You know, we don't serve niggers here." My father said, "Since we aren't niggers, would you mind if we had a cup of coffee and a slice of bread?" The man didn't know what to say, and I guess he said all right, but he was worried about what he'd done. So, when he brought the bread and the cup of coffee, he informed them that they would have to eat outside. Mrs. Bethune said, "Oh, no. We wouldn't have to take it out. We don't have to take it out"— like she didn't know what he was talking about. The counter man said to them, "I'll get in trouble if I serve you in here with white folks." So my father said, "Oh, you don't have to serve us with white people. Do you have a tall glass?" The man said yes. My father said, "Well, you get me the tall glass." And he said, "Dr. Bethune, would you bring the fan?" So she went out to the car and brought in a fan made out of palm leaves. She put the fan down in the glass, and my father said, "Now we're segregated." And the man let them eat! Dad did the same thing in the dining car on the train going to New York with a fan on the table between him and the white person across from him.

In Daytona, I went to school on campus rather than to a local school. This was the pattern everywhere we went. It was dangerous for us to be let out anywhere other than on campus, where we were supervised and protected by the entire faculty. The main reason for caution was fear of what low-class whites might do. But some of the blacks in the community despised people from the campus. Local citizens, very few of whom had any higher education themselves, didn't feel a part of the college. They did not come to events on campus. Also, few from the college faculty attended church out in the community.

Daytona-Cookman had only about three white people on the faculty. I don't think that, as a child, I ever asked the question, "Well, where *are* the white people? Why are there only a few white people here? What are we talking about when we talk about integration?" It was in my brain, but it was something I couldn't pull out. Where were the people like the ones I had to contend with in West Medford?

All of my teachers in the school for faculty children were black when I started in Daytona. That year was perfect, although I was getting a little wild. Then the next year I got in a classroom with a white teacher named Miss French. It was obvious from the moment that I walked in that classroom that she hated me.

The relatively few whites still teaching in black schools by my time were mostly holdovers from the days when the faculties had been predominantly white. Now there were almost enough black college graduates to staff the black schools. The whites who remained seemed to me to attempt a certain elevation from everybody else. I don't remember anybody white ever coming to our house or our going to theirs.

Miss French was teaching a subject that I always excelled in. But she never called on me no matter how many times I'd hold up my hand. She never gave me a decent mark on my papers. I would go home and tell my mother and father how she reacted to me. They couldn't understand it, but they didn't want to confront her.

One day Miss French called me up to the front of the room to read a paper that I had never seen before. In the reading of the paper, I may have skipped a word or didn't pronounce something right. She came up to me and shook me and said, "Don't you *ever* do anything like this again in my classroom!" Well, I didn't know what she was talking about. I didn't know what the word was. Then she told me to continue with the reading. I said, "I'm *not* going to continue with the reading." She said, "You will!" and shook me again. In front of me was a metal folding chair. I banged it across her. She fell down, screaming and hollering.

Well, in those days, anybody who got into trouble had to appear before the student body at its noon meeting. Miss French came limping into the chapel, with someone on each side because I was supposed to have broken her leg, and reported me. She got up and told how I had beaten her with a chair.

My father said, "Miss Peggy Wright come to the front." I went down the aisle. My father said, "You have heard the charge against you. What is your statement?" I said, "Yes, I did it." And I said, "The one thing I am proud of is that I did it this time. I should have done it before." The students applauded! She was so evil! She used her position in subtle ways to put down her students. She was supposed to be such a wonderful Christian person. She probably thought this was a good chance to show these little black children who's in charge, especially if she could do this to the vice president's daughter. So when I got up at this meeting and challenged her and the students clapped, it was sweet revenge. And Miss French didn't act anymore the way she had acted toward me.

My dad was so proud of me he didn't know what to do. I've never had such a wonderful dinner as we had that night. During the meal he talked about the events of the day and about so many other reasons that he was proud of me—things that I had not heard before. It would have been very easy for him to have felt, now, she's put me in an awkward position.

Tuskegee and Talladega

After two years at Daytona-Cookman, my father and mother returned to Tuskegee Institute, where I started my four years of high
school. This was 1926. My father taught English and drama and
acted as assistant dean. My mother was the administrative secretary of the national black Parent-Teacher Association.

Booker T. Washington had died in 1915, and Robert Moton—
like Washington from Hampton Institute in Virginia—was now
Tuskegee's president. Tuskegee was in the process of going one
year at a time to the college level and granting academic degrees.
My dad helped develop the college curriculum. This was happening throughout black education at the time.

Tuskegee's historical role had been to take young people off
the farms and out of the slums and give them a practical education. In the early days, parents brought students to Tuskegee in
about the sixth or the seventh grade, and many of these youngsters remained at Tuskegee—without going home—until they
graduated in four or five years. Their parents didn't have the
money to pay travel expenses. (Even as late as my time, some parents would come in wagons and set up in the "bottom," as we
called it, at graduation.) The students were a bit older for their
grades than students today. They were not children as we now

know them, being more mature and used to hard knocks in the world.

Booker T. Washington and W. E. B. Du Bois had fussed a lot over Tuskegee's (and Hampton Institute's) emphasis on industrial and agricultural training. Du Bois felt that Tuskegee put too much emphasis on the trades and not enough on academics. Tuskegee had more money than most other black colleges because of Booker T. Washington's great fund-raising ability. As a result, Tuskegee had many fine buildings devoted to the trades with faculty to match. If wealthy white people who came down from the North for the winter had something broken, they would send word and a student would go over and mend whatever it was. A lot of those people gave money to the school because of that.

In the late twenties, some of the steam had gone out of the Washington-Du Bois debate. A student could select to go through the trades and graduate or through the academic curriculum and graduate or a combination of the two. The trades, though still strong, were waning. But at every faculty dinner, somebody was either for or against Du Bois.

My parents would be close to Du Bois in years to come, but they straddled the fence between him and Washington. They favored a broad spectrum of education for the black children who came to Tuskegee, most of whom had not had any halfway decent early instruction. They thought you had to put more emphasis on learning than on repairing somebody's steps or somebody's bannister. Tuskegee was not as bad as Hampton because Tuskegee had a nearly all-black staff, while Hampton had more whites, including the president and the heads of departments. Hampton's idea of Du Bois was totally off the window. There was no reason for a lot of book learning. It wouldn't work. We'll put more of our time, energy, and money into training the students to go back and be *leaders* in their communities. Now, Tuskegee was quite different from that. Booker Washington believed in both, although that's not the way he is usually painted.

My mother worked in the same building with George Washington Carver at Tuskegee. I always called George Carver "Doctor Carver." Mom's office was right across the hall from his laboratory. I got to know him well when I stopped in to see my mother after classes. Alabama had a state fair each year in Montgomery, which was not very far from Tuskegee. The fair wanted Dr. Carver to exhibit some of his discoveries, which I believe he had never done before. Black people would be allowed to run the booth. As I remember, ours was the only exhibit by black people at the fair. Dr. Carver selected me, along with a handful of other students, to go to Montgomery and stay with his things and explain them to the public. Dr. Carver told us all about sweet potatoes and peanuts. He had also developed a lot of dyes, which we were supposed to demonstrate. But Dr. Carver was at the booth so much of the time that I didn't get much chance to answer anybody's question!

To the young people on campus, Dr. Carver was not the man who came to be known around the world. Nobody ever told us much about his greatness. He was a very queer individual, isolated in his office. He had nothing to do with anything on campus. He was single and getting crotchety. We thought of him as elderly, though he wasn't really, and a nuisance. We felt that he was a meddler. If he met us at the post office, he would want to know why we were there and what we were up to. If we didn't say it right, he would tell our parents. He was kind of a grandfather in reverse.

I had never even gone to the state fair before, so this was exciting. In fact, the only time my family and I ever got to Montgomery was when Tuskegee played Montgomery State in football. We didn't go anywhere. Tuskegee was a world unto itself. I didn't know anything about the stores or have any desire to go to Montgomery even though it was only thirty-five miles away.

Tuskegee Institute was a large school with a famous football team and facilities that white colleges could have envied. Edward Waters and Daytona-Cookman were in an entirely different league. My family lived on what was called "Wicker Row." The institute had built three new houses for faculty members side by side outside the college gate, and all of us had wicker furniture in the living room. We socialized exclusively with black people at the college, as well as with the doctors at a new black Veterans Hospital down the road and their families. Generally you had no racial viciousness at Tuskegee because white people didn't live anywhere near the campus. I do remember one exception, though.

A white man came to our house in Tuskegee to see my father and called him "Johnny." He was looking for John C. Wright, but he couldn't say "Mr. Wright" or "John C. Wright" or "Dr. Wright." I said, "Johnny does not live here." So the man left. I knew he was going to come back because I saw him cross the street to the funeral parlor to ask where my father lived. The man did come back, and I got the tea kettle full of boiling water. I went on the porch, and I told him that if he put his foot up on that step that I was going to drown him with scalding water. That was one time I had to face a situation where I had to make a decision about "do you accept or not."

Tuskegee had a cultural life unlike most of Alabama or the South. A tradition had started with Booker T. Washington. He had all sorts of contacts with people in the arts, and many of them wanted to come down to Tuskegee. They brought plays and musicals—oh my goodness—and opera and ballet. Top actors and actresses from Broadway, both white and black, but mostly white, came all the time. A special train would bring them the five miles from Chehaw, the nearest stop on the main line. We had all of this long before most black people ever saw a play or ballet.

We had a fancy dining room at Tuskegee for the performers. The best food in the world was served there—fricasseed chicken and whatever they had in big-city restaurants. That was training for students in Tuskegee's Home Economics Department. We faculty children tried as hard as we could to get to work in this dining room. (We would have our friends under the windows so we could drop extra food down to them.) The dining room the performers used was set apart out of public view. Blacks and whites who came down as a group from the North could eat here together. There would be no one to object. Sitting together publicly in the chapel was another matter.

During the winter, the wealthy white people who came down from the North attended chapel to hear the wonderful singing. The same had been true at Daytona-Cookman. These white visitors had seats on the stage, separated from all the black people. A lot of adult blacks objected to this segregation on their own campus. I myself accepted it as just the way things were. It didn't interfere with anything I wanted to do. But then I was young and didn't yet see clearly what segregation meant.

We faculty children went, marched actually, to chapel on Sunday, rather than to a church in town. Chapel was mandatory. An Episcopal priest, a young white man, came each Sunday afternoon to teach Sunday school in one of the academic buildings. The man could not have done better if he had given each one of us a fur coat. We couldn't get away from our families on Sunday very well, so all of us just jumped at this great opportunity. For us it was a joyride because we could legitimately meet with boyfriends, even stop by the drug store on the way. And the priest liked us. He was enthusiastic about everything. That had an impact on us. I don't believe we learned much about the Episcopal Church. We learned a lot about the Bible. Once a month he would have a communion service.

My high school education at Tuskegee was entirely on the academic side of the curriculum. I studied languages, math, English, chemistry, and physics, just like students do today. These were happy years. I was a "good" student with occasional lapses. One time I was reading a book for teenagers called *Bad Girl*, which sounds provocative, but it wasn't. We had this great speaker at weekday chapel, who had been to India and done many good works. But I had *Bad Girl* with me, and I was absorbed in it while this wonderful speaker was addressing us. All of a sudden I thought I heard the people clapping. So I clapped. But the speech was still going on, and they came and dragged me out of there!

As I neared the end of my high school years, my parents loosened the reins a bit. I was a good dancer, and they would let me go to faculty dances. I would partner with the young faculty guys. That was great because they could really dance, too. My parents also—reluctantly—let me go to parties at the home of a Mrs. Clark, whose husband taught in the automotive trades. Mom and Dad would discuss Mrs. Clark with other parents at bridge parties. They could never decide to say "no" to my going but were always on the verge of it.

At Mrs. Clark's, we played records of the latest black music and really danced. You were spinning around and falling back and shaking and it was hot! But Mrs. Clark had nonalcoholic punch, and I don't remember anybody slipping behind the bushes for a drink, either. And actually there wasn't a lot of romancing. More little sparks than anything else. But lots of dancing.

My life at Tuskegee would soon change. My father was offered the presidency of the Joseph K. Brick Agricultural, Industrial, and Normal School at Bricks, North Carolina, near Rocky Mount. My brother John was already at Morehouse College in Atlanta. The rest of my family left me at Tuskegee shortly before my graduation from high school and moved to Bricks—in the fateful year of 1929. I would visit in the summer.

The student population at Brick School was heavily Northern. The families of some of the students worked for wealthy white people, particularly in New Jersey and New York. The Congregational Church, through the American Missionary Association (or Aunt Mary Ann) underwrote Brick, along with numerous other schools throughout the South. The AMA-supported institutions were now advancing to the college level. The church knew of Dad when he was at Edward Waters and Bethune-Cookman and wanted him to develop the college curriculum at Brick, as he had helped do at Tuskegee.

My father would send encouraging letters to me from Brick, sometimes including a poem. In one letter that survives, written on the notepaper of the president's home, Trailsend, he wrote, "I guess it is well that you are not with me all of the time. It would be too hard then to give you up when somebody else comes to claim you." Then he added a poem, "You and To-day," written by Ella Wheeler Wilcox:

> With every rising sun
> Think of your life as just begun.

Peggy and a friend at the beach; courtesy of the author.

The past has shrived and buried deep
All yesterdays—there let them sleep,
Nor seek to summon back one ghost
Of that innumerable host.
Concern yourself with but today;
Woo it and teach it to obey
Your wish and will. Since time began
Today has been the friend of man.
But in his blindness and his sorrow
He looks to yesterday and to-morrow.
You and today! a soul sublime
And the great pregnant hour of time.
With God between to bind the twain
Go forth, I say, attain! attain!

This well reflected Dad's attitude toward me. Particularly the expectation that I would "attain! attain!"

To jump ahead, all Dad's work at Brick would come crashing down in 1933, the depth of the Depression. There would be no money to pay the teachers, and the Congregational Church would close the school, leaving the Wright family stranded.

After Mom and Dad left for Brick, I finished high school and then entered the first year of college at Tuskegee. That would have been 1930. I moved into the girls' dormitory next to the home of Tuskegee's president Robert Moton. I was an unofficial member of Dr. Moton's household. The Motons, who had several children, also unofficially adopted a boy from East St. Louis, Missouri, named Herman Green. He was my main boyfriend in my Tuskegee years, on and off.

Herman's mother had brought him down to Tuskegee when he was in the seventh grade, probably to get him out of the slums.

Tuskegee was well known in East St. Louis, and several students attended from there. Herman was unusually handsome. He became an outstanding basketball player. The girls in the Moton family took an interest in him, and so did I. My parents, before they left, knew that I had a crush on the young man and laid down the law that he could not come to our house and sit on the porch at night. For a while Herman would be my boyfriend, and for a while the boyfriend of my roommate Mary Taylor. It would be Mary this semester and Peggy the next, but, in the end, Mary and Herman got married. I had other boyfriend interests in the off semesters, particularly a boy named Dumas from New Orleans and a boy named Mazake from Mississippi. They were both "wealthy" in the sense that they didn't have to have financial aid to attend college.

We girls walked up a hill to classes from our dormitory. Along the way, we picked up the boys at the corner of their dormitory, and they walked with us. We would let them know quite loudly that we were walking by. We were forever finding ways to stay on the top of that hill with our boyfriends. The gate to get off the campus was not very far. Girls could walk up to the gate but not pass though it. Boys could go through the gate and out into the town.

In the summer it was different. Somebody would get a car, usually the son of Tuskegee's vice president Harold Logan. My group would be off to Chehaw, the rail siding on the main line, by the Chehaw River. We weren't supposed to go, which made it all the more fun. There we would swim all afternoon and have the best time in the world.

We had a short break in the middle of the school day at Tuskegee. We would eat lunch as quickly as possible and get back to the main building where they had a piano. Teddy Wilson, a great fellow who went on to be a famous jazzman, played that piano while we danced. Teddy's father taught in the engineering program, and his mother also taught. Teddy would go out to Chehaw with us. The thing to understand is that black musicians like Teddy Wilson played many of the same songs that white America was listening to, but they played them *black.* There was more swing to the song when a black person was playing for a black audience, which was exciting then. "Baby Face," "Sleepy-time Gal," or whatever would come out differently from the way it did when whites played it. "Bye, Bye Blackbird" was a favorite at Tuskegee. When President Moton, who was dark skinned, left for a trip, students would strike this up! Which was terrible, but tells you something about color consciousness.

Skin color could come up in unexpected ways. The school decided that it would like to have "Miss Tuskegee." So they had an election, and I won. This was the first year, as far as I know, that they had selected a Miss Tuskegee. The first big duty of the winner was to represent the school at a football game in Chicago. My uncle in Newark heard about this. He went to a department store and bought a suitcase full of clothes for me to carry to Chicago for this great occasion. Before the football game, there was a parade on campus, which I led. On the day that the football team was to leave, I packed my bag and went down to the station with the rest of the people who were going and waited for the train to take us to Chehaw and on to Chicago.

Captain Neeley, who was in charge of discipline on campus, came down to the siding just before the train left and said, "Peggy, I have to tell you that you cannot be Miss Tuskegee at the football game in Chicago. I have decided that it would be better if you remained on campus." The shock was terrific, but this was Captain Neeley, and his word was law. I said, "I'm ready to go. My suitcase is packed. What should I do?" He said, "Nothing. You're just not going." He never gave a reason, just, "You're not going." I didn't have the courage to challenge him, but I strongly suspected the real reason. Captain Neeley was about the darkest person on Tuskegee's campus, and my family was light. He never liked any of us, and I think this had a lot to do with it.

While I was in my freshman and sophomore years at Tuskegee, I decided that I wanted to pursue modern dance. The nearest college that offered what I wanted was Talladega College, which had an excellent physical education program including both sports and dancing. Talladega was a small black school, supported by the Congregational Church, about eighty miles north of Tuskegee near Birmingham. (The Congregational Church, which selected my father for Brick, helped him with my tuition.) Somebody suggested that I should go to Simmons in Massachusetts. I wasn't interested in Simmons. I wanted to go where black people were. So I decided to go to Talladega.

Today there is a well-known speedway near Talladega, Alabama, but then it didn't exist. Talladega was an isolated spot, entirely different from Tuskegee. You had to *go* to Talladega. The town of Talladega was a "redneck" place with the lowest kind of people—and very racist. Ignorant racism. The workers in the textile factory there were upset to see black students dressed well. Fortunately the town was separated from the college. In fact, college officials would not permit the students to walk through the town. We had to take a path around the town itself because the locals probably would have attempted to harm us.

Talladega, unlike Tuskegee, was a scholastic institution. You didn't play around. You went there to get your education. It was one of the black schools that had come up out of the sand to become a real college. Talladega, unlike Tuskegee, had a fairly large percentage of white people on the faculty. The president of Talladega was Buell Gallagher, a white man. He had headed a white prep school in New Jersey named Blair Academy. My dad, years before, had taught at Blair in the summer and knew Gallagher. Talladega did not have the same huge financial support from the North that Tuskegee had. This was an especially acute problem because, with the deepening of the Depression, Talladega's enrollment had fallen off in 1932, when I arrived, from roughly three hundred to two hundred students.

My interest in dance, which took me to Talladega, was an interest in *modern* dance, and particularly Martha Graham. While I was at Tuskegee, Martha Graham and other dance troupes performed there. Those of us who seemed to have some talent would be invited to join the troupe during its visit. It was wonderful and captured my imagination. My father wasn't too happy about this development. But he couldn't object too much because, at that time, Martha Graham had a religious aspect. Her dances would be done in churches as part of worship services, and I would do this myself in years to come. At Tuskegee other students and I would perform Martha Graham dances at the black Veterans Hospital.

Along with dance and my other studies at Talladega, I did what college students do, Depression or no Depression. I was not a person who made friends too readily, but I pledged a sorority, Delta Sigma Theta. I was accepted and went "on line." That's what they called it when you have to do two or three weeks of bidding of your sorority. My roommate, who was from Tuskegee but went to Talladega as a freshman, was already in the Delta. She knew all about me. She knew that I could not eat greasy food, so they got hold of a half-quart of mayonnaise that had spoiled. My task was to eat the whole jar.

It pretty near killed me. I passed out, and everybody got

afraid. They knew that they couldn't call the hospital for fear of getting in trouble. Fortunately, the president's wife heard about it and said, "Bring her here." She sent for the doctor. Later Mrs. Gallagher said, "Peggy, if you want to be in the sorority, it's okay with me. But you are not to do anything else on this line. If they don't understand it, you have them come to me." She kept me at her house throughout the rest of the time students were on line. But they did take me into the sorority.

On Saturday at Talladega you would go to a social hall where they had a big room with lots of wooden chairs. You would claim your spot and arrange the chairs so you'd have the most private place possible in the room. On Sunday from three to five o'clock, the girls and fellows would meet there and then go to the dining room together. Everybody dressed up for these occasions.

Lots of times I would be meeting Herbert Pigrom from Bessemer, Alabama, a star football player everybody called "Dizzy." He was a bright young man, who planned to go to medical school. Dizzy had been at Tuskegee before Talladega, as I had. He was quiet and appeared to be much older than the other students in his class.

Even though I enjoyed my school work, I didn't care too much for Talladega. One reason was that everybody had to wait on tables in the dining room. Each semester you got a chart, and you had so many tables that you waited. I didn't want to do that. My roommate, who was from Atlanta and the daughter of a wealthy physician, didn't want to do it either. I figured that I didn't go to Talladega to learn how to wait on tables. I went there because I wanted a college education, and whatever interfered with it, I wasn't too happy about.

Dizzy was quite understanding of my lack of enthusiasm for

waiting on tables. He helped me through those bitter days. In fact, he offered, on days that I felt that I just could not do it, to wait in my place. If I really had a bad attitude about it, Dizzy would say, "Now Peggy, you sit over there at my table, and I'll wait your table this time." I have a picture of the two of us under a tree. When you stopped at a tree at Talladega, that meant you're engaged. That's what the picture was all about.

At least that's what it was supposed to mean. Dizzy was serious. I was not serious, but I had no real interest in anybody at that time. He graduated the year before I did, but he came back from Bessemer on weekends in my senior year. It was a pretty done deal as far as his folks and mine were concerned. He applied to go to the black med school called Meharry in Nashville. He did not get a scholarship and was unable to go. The public school in Bessemer had its eyes on him to coach the basketball and football teams. Dizzy had a promise from the school that it would have an opening for me, too. But that's not how things worked out.

$\underset{\curlyveedownarrow}{\diamondsuit}$

Atlanta

While I was posing under the tree at Talladega, Brick School up in North Carolina failed. Unfortunately none of the black colleges in the South were looking for a president. Most of the "slots" were taken. The Congregational Church could not find a place for my father that would be up to his standards. But someone in the American Missionary Association knew someone in the YMCA, where Dad, of course, also had contacts. The director of the Y and pastor of the First Congregational Church in Atlanta had been called to the faculty of Fisk University. These jobs were then offered to Dad.

Reluctantly, and scared, Dad accepted the First Congregational pulpit (and temporarily the Atlanta Y). He had no training in theology. But he accepted the challenge. He audited courses at the Theological School in Atlanta, and he remained at the church until his death in 1946. He also wrote a column, called "From My Study Window," for Atlanta's black newspaper, the *Daily World*. In one column in 1944, he would sound a theme that became important in my own life: "We find that the cruelest of all the discriminations which are practiced against colored workers in this country is the refusal to upgrade them in their work; to recognize and reward ability and loyalty when it is found in a black skin. The typically American story of black workers would record them as ending just where they started. Once a porter, always a porter; once a janitor at twelve dollars a week, always a janitor; . . . once a dining car waiter . . . always a dining car waiter."[1]

The First Congregational Church—located two blocks from famous Auburn Avenue—was *the* black church in terms of status in Atlanta. It was also the church attended by many of the students in the several black colleges in Atlanta. The black people who had position and money belonged to First Congregational. The name of the church ate on the soul of white Atlanta. It was called the "First" Congregational Church, and black people didn't have the *first* of anything! Sometimes white people came there for my father to marry them not knowing that this was an all-black church. Occasionally someone would say, "Just marry us anyway. I don't care." But he could never do that because it would have caused an explosion.

Services at First Congregational were different from those at many other black churches in Atlanta. They started at eleven o'clock on the dot. Everybody was seated. There were few stragglers. To be an usher at First Congregational was really fine. Graham Jackson—the one who would later play the accordion when FDR died—was the organist. You went to your pew, and I mean you went to *your* pew, which might have been in the family for generations. The other black churches had *extended* services. The singing was beautiful, but they went on and on and on. They were usually out around two o'clock, while First Congregational finished at twelve or twelve-thirty.

1. J. C. Wright, "From My Study Window: Started at the Bottom," (Atlanta, Ga.) *Daily World,* Sunday, May 21, 1944.

Addie Streator Wright on her way to the First Congregational Church in Atlanta; courtesy of the author.

There was no emotionalism at First Congregational. Sometimes the older parishioners would say, "That's right. That's right." But not often. If you did that once or twice and had the people turn and look at you, you didn't do it again. That wasn't the way it worked, and the church was quite proud of it. I don't like to use the word "snobbish," but we were.

But this is jumping ahead a little bit. From Talladega, I went to Atlanta by way of Miami. Dad—my chief planner, I'll say it like that—had lined up a job for me teaching phys ed at Booker T. Washington Senior High School in Miami. Recently built Booker T. Washington School was the first black high school in that part of Florida, and it became famous all over the state. One historian has called it "the intellectual seat of black Miami." That may be, but when I went there in 1934 I didn't see it in such a rosy light.

No sooner had I settled into my boarding house and started work than I found that there were certain things that I would have to do in order to maintain my position. In those days, if you were on the federal or state payroll, there was often something going on under the table. At Booker T. Washington, it was the "examination on call." In other words, you would get the teachers' examination not in writing but on call. I got uneasy about that. It was hanky-panky. I will arrange for you, young lady, if you do this for me. It wasn't long before I realized that I had to get out of there in order to keep my reputation.

I also arrived at the high school when native-born students and immigrants, mostly from the Bahamas, were at each other's throats. The local people resented the newcomers because they would come over and take the top jobs and excel at school. The immigrants tended to be lighter skinned than the native-born, giving the immigrants a leg up. This was an irritant, too. War broke out between the two groups. The violence, with guns and knives, was something that you wouldn't believe.

I was in the middle of the strife because the other phys ed teacher, who was to be the football coach, backed out at the last minute. The principal of Booker T. Washington said that he would appoint me as the head of the whole physical education program and that I had to take the responsibility of the football team! He didn't give me an opportunity to say, "No way in the world I can do anything like that. I don't know enough about it."

But Miami was not entirely bad. I loved the girls' phys ed program, even though I had to teach all the grades together. When they let the girls out, it was usually when the boys got out, and you had at least five or six classes in one area. This was an explosive mixture. I would stand up on a platform and show them tap dancing and attempt to have organization in the groups. But if anybody said something about somebody else, there might have been riot.

After about three months of the threat of examination on call and the student warfare and the overwhelming phys ed assignment, my father came down to Miami, rescued me, and took me to Atlanta. The experience in Miami had been so bruising that I had to be hospitalized "for relaxation" until I bounced back.

Thanks to the First Congregational Church, my family had a lovely home in an exclusive part of the black community in Atlanta—Johnson Avenue and later Angier Avenue. Atlanta had several black colleges—Spelman, Morehouse, Morris-Brown, Atlanta University—and a substantial black upper class, including quite a few black doctors. Which reminds me of the medical situation for blacks at the time.

It was a fight to get black people admitted into Atlanta's Grady Hospital. In the early 1940s, my mother would be diagnosed with cancer. She had a female doctor and a male doctor, both black, who belonged to our church. Neither of them could get her into Grady. There was a hospital for black people at Tuskegee with several doctors on staff. The administration told Mom that she could be admitted. She ultimately went to Tuskegee for her operation, which was not successful.

You wouldn't have dared have anybody except a black doctor. I don't know whether the white doctors would treat any of us, but I doubt it. One of the black doctors, a friend of ours who belonged to our church, had a hospital in a big house. It was not a "recognized" hospital. It was a place to go when you were sick and hope that you came out of it alive! This was the sort of place that blacks went, both in Atlanta and elsewhere in the South.

I went to this unofficial hospital for my "relaxation" and on another occasion. I had an appendicitis. Mom took me there for the operation. I remember it well because I was recuperating at the time of the World Series. I loved baseball and followed it all the time on the radio. My mother said to the doctor, "Now don't forget that Peggy wants to be sure to hear the World Series." The doctor said to my mother, "Addie, she can only go home on one condition. You have an ironing board, don't you?" My mother said, "Sure." He said, "Well, you take one of the nurses home and you strap Peggy to the ironing board and put it across two chairs in the living room and she can listen to the Series. Then afterwards, bring her back for me to check on her." And that's what we did.

We lived near John Wesley Dobbs, one of the top leaders in Atlanta's black community, and his family. They were members of our church. All of Mr. Dobbs's several daughters sang in the choir. He was a postman, and, at that time, that was high employment for blacks. He owned his house, his wife didn't have to work outside the home, and all of his children went to college. His daughter Mattiwilda became famous as a singer and moved to Sweden. All of the girls had beautiful voices, and they were gorgeous. Mr. Dobbs believed in their eating plenty. The oldest Dobbs daughter, Irene, was the mother of Maynard Jackson, who became mayor of Atlanta in the 1970s.

In Atlanta the exclusive neighborhoods were just a short walk from Auburn Avenue, the black Main Street, which we called "the strip." Ma Sutton had a beautiful restaurant on Auburn Avenue. There was another high-class one called the Metropolitan. But there were also a lot of joints on Auburn Avenue. If you really wanted to get a feel of Auburn Avenue, you'd go in quietly and sit in the back of one of these spots. My mother would walk down Bell Street to get to Auburn Avenue. The people on Bell Street were known to play the numbers. She knew all the people there. Very few blacks of social standing would be seen on Bell Street—daytime or night. Bell Street coexisted with other elements near Auburn Avenue, but you'd always ask, "Which church do you belong to?" That was a marker.

The First Congregational Church was near Auburn Avenue. Close by were the other two big black churches in Atlanta, a Methodist and a Baptist—Ebenezer Baptist, whose minister was Martin Luther King, Sr., a shouting and clapping sort of preacher. The churchgoing blacks were primarily congregated in this one area—poor and rich alike—on Sunday morning. They would go up the steps into these churches with their big hats and gloves, even if the finery had to be paid for from the rent money. All black. No whites anywhere on Auburn Avenue.

Atlanta was a segregated city in the 1930s. Almost everything was separate. You didn't get used to it, but, by the same token, you couldn't fight it every hour of the day. Segregation was a part of life, and you had to work around it as best you could.

I had to go back and forth across town every day to my job, which I'll shortly describe. My older brother attended Atlanta University, and my younger brother was now at Morehouse. But we didn't have the money for all three of us to take the streetcar. My brothers started out ahead of me on foot. I took the streetcar and had to sit in the "colored" section at the rear—or stand in the colored section even if seats were free to the front. When this streetcar got to a certain stop, John or Herb would be waiting. I would drop my transfer ticket out the window to whichever brother got there first so he could then take that ticket and go on across town on another streetcar to his college. I might have been in the second-class section, but this is the *best* place to drop that transfer out of the window. So I got back at the system of segregation at least in this small way. Segregation kept me out of the seats up front, but I helped my brothers get through college!

In the stores, if you were black, you could not try on dresses or hats unless the store owner knew who you were and where you came from. I made $13.00 a week at my job, but I had a charge account at Muse's Department Store. This was the most expensive of the stores in Atlanta, and an exception to the rule. There I could try on a dress and stand out in the center of the room and see how I looked, rather than having to stay behind curtains. Unlike many other stores, Muse's had no "colored" here and "white" here. You paid the price of the dress or the hat or the shoes, and you got the same thing as a white person. You could try on a dress in a little changing room. You could come out to the center of the main room and be able to see in the mirrors all around. But the clothes cost a lot more than at Rich's, another big department store in Atlanta. If you had a charge account at other stores, they would let you try on a hat or a dress, but there were little closet-like places for blacks to do this. You could not come out in the open to get a good look at whatever you were thinking of buying. That was the difference. But you paid for that privilege at Muse's.

Most of my purchases at Muse's were actually for my mother. (She wouldn't enter the store herself because money was tight, and she couldn't bring herself to go into debt even one penny.) Some women in the church would say behind Mom's back, "She's not satisfied unless she has on a pair of shoes from Muse's," meaning she was putting on airs by wearing expensive shoes. If I heard these remarks, I would say to them, "How did you manage at Rich's where you had to be segregated in order to buy? Now what did you do?" Of course, everybody suffered from segregation whether they shopped at Muse's or Rich's. You handled it the way *you* had to handle it.

My job in Atlanta was with the Federal Emergency Relief Administration, or FERA. This was one of the original New Deal programs, to be replaced in 1935 by the WPA. I was hired as a social worker even though I had no professional training. Along with the school system, the FERA became one of the main sources of professional jobs for educated black people in Atlanta. FERA broke precedent by having whites and blacks work together in the same office instead of having their separate units. Our headquarters was located near Atlanta University.

My caseload at first consisted of homeless black men in the center of town. Many of them lived in carriage houses or garages behind the mansions white people had abandoned. Their rent was subsidized by the FERA. When my mother learned about my caseload, she said, "How much are you making a week?" I said, "Thirteen dollars." And she said with an exasperated sigh, "That'll never get a car and a driver, and you're not going on these cases in that area by yourself." So she said, "I will pay somebody to drive you there and sit at each entrance." What she did was to get a young man who drove a Cadillac—off the junk heap—to sit at the end of the alleyway and wait for me when I paid my case visits. I would go all the way down the alley, and he would drive around and meet me at the other end. I was humiliated that my mother had done that, but she said, "Now that's the *only* way that you're going to work there."

At first Mom came too. Then, as I emerged from my visits to clients not crying or anything, she felt maybe this was going to work. She sat in the car, but sometimes she would walk behind me, not for my protection, but to meet these guys. She usually had some cookies and sometimes an apple pie for the men. They all knew Mrs. Wright. Everybody accepted that this was Addie Streator Wright. This is the way she performed. She was a classic.

Part of my responsibility was to get the men employable. But this was in the depth of the Depression and people with college degrees could not get jobs. Many of my clients were from the Carribean and could not speak English well enough to have held a job anyway. I had to see if the relief that my client got was sufficient to pay the rent and, if he had a family somewhere else, if that family needed money to survive. Some from the Carribean were sending money back to their home countries, and many of them that did would send so much that, by the end of the month, they had nothing. But these were the greatest guys I've ever worked with, and in years to come I drew on this experience.

Later the FERA had me work in a different part of town with black families, rather than men living singly. The poverty was appalling. It came about because of the Depression, but it was also simply a continuation of the way blacks were always treated. I realized that I needed to have more education if I were to address what I saw. Fortunately, the Congregational Church stepped forward, as it did so often for Wrights, to give me a two-year scholarship in the School of Social Work on the campus of Atlanta University, now Clark Atlanta University.

In the mid 1920s, sociologist E. Franklin Frazier had directed the School of Social Work, but the institution's first real growth occurred under his successor, Forrester B. Washington, who headed the school when I was there. Most of my courses, such as psychopathology and techniques of social investigation, were the same as those in a white school, I am sure. Some, such as Industrial Problems of the Negro and Recreational Leadership and the Negro, were not.

But, again, I am a little ahead of my story. The year before I entered the School of Social Work, a young man by the name of Frank Tucker Wood Jr., a graduate of North Carolina Agricultural and Technical College, preceded me. Frank had majored in agriculture at A&T, which is what you did at A&T. But after college he decided that he wanted to be in some form of social work. He received a scholarship to the School of Social Work and joined our church. My Lord! My father thought that he was the greatest thing since rice.

Frank came from Virginia. His ancestors were enslaved on a plantation in Gloucester County, Virginia, on a point of land called Ware Neck off Chesapeake Bay, not too far from Yorktown. After emancipation, the Wood family, including Frank's grandmother, a Powhatan Indian, continued to live on Ware Neck. The little community where Frank was born in 1910 was called Ark.

Peggy's report card from the Atlanta School of Social Work, 1938; courtesy of the author.

Frank was the oldest in a family of seven boys. Frank's father—the last of fourteen children—was a carpenter and farmer. Frank's mother was very Indian-looking. Of the seven boys, they hit everything, dark, light, Indian, you name it. Everybody down in that part of Virginia was Baptist, and the Woods were no exception. They were big supporters of the Union Zion Baptist Church in their neighborhood.

All but one of the seven Wood boys graduated from college. This is amazing when you consider that their father could not read or write and when you consider the limited opportunities for black people in rural Virginia. College education was typical of both my family and Frank's. But the attitude was different. With the Wrights, the focus was on schooling. With the Woods, it was on religion. Also the two families viewed college education in a different light. Frank's mother and father saw college as a place for their children to *make* it. But I grew up with college just happening, with no thought of anything different.

Frank went through the sixth grade on Ware Neck, and then he moved to his Aunt Daisy's in Norfolk, Virginia. He lived there with her until he graduated from Norfolk's Booker T. Washington High School. In 1929, A&T in Greensboro, North Carolina, offered him a scholarship. He was elected president of the student body at A&T, but he didn't have enough money to go to school continuously. He had to stay out a year and work. His job that year was as a sailor for the Merchants and Miners Transportation Company, which owned a fleet of ships carrying passengers and freight up and down the East Coast.

The first year Frank was in Atlanta, he and I were not really friends. I thought he was too self-important. Everybody at the church made over him, and I guess I didn't feel very happy about that. He had what my father thought was just about the greatest talent of anybody. But by the next year when I also entered the School of Social Work, I had another look at Frank. We took classes together and became a couple by the time he graduated. While this was going on, I gradually parted from Herbert Pigrom, the fellow I had dated in Talladega.

This development with Frank was not to my parents' liking. They had plans for me! My father had spoken with the administrator of a black social service agency in Philadelphia about a job for me as a social worker. Also talked about was the possibility that I might take a masters degree in public health from New York University. A recruiter for the Georgia State Office of Health had tentatively offered a scholarship for me to do this. But in a conference with Forester Washington, head of the School of Social Work, and the recruiter, Forester said, "Peggy, you have not said anything about your relationship with Frank Wood." I said, "No, I haven't." I said it like I didn't think it was particularly the recruiter's business. She said right away, "Oh well, that's a good question. What *are* your intentions?" I said, "I don't know. We haven't gotten that far." The recruiter said, "I must tell you before we go any further that, if you marry, you cannot have the scholarship or the job." And she said, "You really have to give this good thought. I'm fifty-five years old, and I have worked for this agency all these years. I am *never* going to be able to marry because no one is going to be interested in me when I leave state employment." It was a shock because I was thinking that I could see New York City and get a masters degree and come back. Forester said, "Peggy, you know that you're not going to want this. If I were you, I would not take it." So I turned that down.

But Frank and I as a couple didn't please my parents for another reason. My father had cooled toward Frank. Dad had a high view of the qualifications required to marry his daughter, and

Frank didn't have them! My mother thought pretty much of Frank, but even her enthusiasm had waned. Number one, Frank didn't have any money, and he didn't come from a family with any money. Number two, he had taken a lowly job out of the School for Social Work.

Frank's lowly job, as a way-down-the-list insurance agent, was actually arranged by my dad. Dad was close to the family who owned North Carolina Mutual Life Insurance Company. That was "the" insurance company for black people. In 1937 North Carolina Mutual found a position for Frank in Chattanooga, Tennessee, until he got something in social work. In Chattanooga Frank had to go from house to house collecting the few coins people put in envelopes to pay their premiums for what they thought of as their burial insurance.

With the Philadelphia job still on the table and Frank off in Chattanooga, it looked like Frank's and my relationship might be coming to an end. Probably my father had that in mind also! At this point, though, Frank and I decided that the best thing for us was to get married. Most of that came from me because I saw myself otherwise packing my bags for Philadelphia.

It had begun to be whispered around in church that Frank and Peggy would probably be getting married. Nothing was said openly, but Frank and I knew my parents were not in favor of our getting married. One time we tried to bring up the subject around the dinner table with my family. That was a mistake! Mom and Dad, and my brothers as well, were having none of it. And Frank had to leave town with nothing settled. This time around the dinner table played a big part in our getting married because he knew that my parents would never agree.

Because of the hard times, my dad had made it known that he would rather not preside at a fancy wedding in the First Congregational Church. There were those few people in the church who, even though it was the Depression, had plenty of money. They could afford a lavish wedding, but Dad would not go along. He planned out a simple, inexpensive ceremony. The bride and groom would come in from separate doors and stand before him. The flowers would be the regular flowers that the church had every Sunday. No bridesmaids, no groomsmen. That was his standard procedure to keep people from wasting the little money they had. But somehow or other, he never saw anything for me but a great big wedding. Maybe if Frank and I had put the emphasis on the lovely wedding, things might have turned out better!

So we decided we would just get married, not tell anybody, and accept the consequences. And, on June 7, 1937, we did. Frank and I had a friend who was a young minister at Gammon, a seminary in Atlanta. The guy did not want to conduct a ceremony for us because he didn't want to get into difficulty with my father. But finally he agreed to perform the ceremony at his house. None of our friends or family members came to the wedding—not even my brothers and sister—because we didn't want anybody to know.

This was entirely different from anything I had done before with my family. We Wrights always discussed important decisions as a group. Everyone participated. I was also going against the wishes of my father, which is something I rarely did.

Before leaving my house on Angier Avenue, I put on a white linen suit. I went in the kitchen and sat while my mother was at the sink because I knew that she always took her ring off when she washed the dishes. And she did. I figured this was a good opportunity to get the ring. She always forgot her ring. Somebody had to remind her of where she put it. When Mom finished the dishes and left the room, I took the ring. From there I went over to the minis-

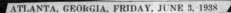

Marriage Announced On
Day Of Her Graduation

MRS. FRANK T. WOOD, JR.

—the former Miss Peggy Addilee Wright, daughter of Rev. and Mrs.
John Clarence Wright of the First Congregational Church, whose marriage to Mr. Frank Tucker Wood, Jr., has just been announced by her
parents.

Mrs. Wood is a graduate of Talladega College and received her
diploma from the Atlanta School of Social Work Thursday evening
while Mr. Wood, an alumnus of Agricultural and Technical College,
Greensboro, N. C., graduated from the Atlanta School of Social Work
last spring. Both young people have been effective leaders in social,
educational, and religious affairs of the city.

Mr. and Mrs. Wood, who are members of the Alpha Phi Alpha fraternity and Delta Sigma Theta sorority, respectively, will be at ho:
in Lima, Ohio, where the former is executive secretary of the Bradford
Community Center, after June 8.

Atlanta Journal *article announcing Peggy's
marriage, June 3, 1938; courtesy of the author.*

ter's house for the marriage ceremony. We stayed until dark. Then Frank left town, and I went home and returned the ring to the kitchen.

Some months went by and it became clear that I had to tell my parents. I told my mother first. I asked her to meet me for a cup of coffee. She had guessed our secret. Mom had always been on my side in everything that happened in the family. She would stand up for me. But this time she didn't. She said, "You knew how it would hurt your father. You knew your father would never under-stand." She kept saying, "Peggy, how in the world could you do this?" She said, "You don't have any money. Frank doesn't have any money. How could you do it?" I said, "Mom, I always knew that you would stand by me and help me through anything I had to do." She said, "But I didn't help you do this." I said, "Yes you did. Your wedding ring! When you took your wedding ring off and left it by the side of the dish water, I knew I could get that ring and take it the night that I got married."

My father almost died. It took him quite a while to get over it, but he eventually did because I was his favorite person. For *me* to have done anything like that was just beyond him. I remember breaking the news to him. The family came together at the table. I asked my father, if I told him something that he was not in favor of, could we discuss it, regardless of how he felt about it. He said, "Peg, I know what you're going to tell me. You're going to tell me that you and Frank got married, and I am not happy about it at all. I am not happy because you had a future by yourself—not with somebody else. And now it means that whatever your future is, you have to be guided by his decisions, and I'm not satisfied with that—not after *all* that we have been able to do."

PART TWO

The Black Community Center

✿

Lima

By the time I graduated from the School of Social Work in June of 1938, Frank had left Chattanooga and taken a job as director of the Bradfield Community Center in Lima, Ohio. Frank had learned about the opening in Lima from Maidie Ruth Gamble, whose father was on the Bradfield center's board. Frank had gotten to know Maidie Ruth in Greensboro. She attended Bennett College while he was at A&T. (Later, as Maidie Norman, she would gain a national reputation as an actress, particularly in movies, including *What Ever Happened to Baby Jane?*) It is only a small exaggeration to say that black college graduates back in the 1930s all knew or knew of each other. Word of job openings passed quickly, as it did from Maidie Ruth to Frank, on this grapevine.

I joined Frank in Lima, happy about his being out of the insurance business, but not so happy about where I found myself. I didn't like Lima very much. Even though it was in the North, it was quite a segregated little town. Lima wasn't much different from the South. The chief employer there was the Lima Locomotive Works. Lima was within driving distance of Detroit, Michigan. That didn't affect *us* because we hardly had the money to drive across town.

Black people in Lima made up about 10 percent of the population. Schools were not segregated by law, as I recall, but the same thing was achieved with the "neighborhood school" concept. I cannot remember having gone to a restaurant. This could have had more to do with finances than segregation. We didn't have the money to go to a restaurant unless they gave away the hot dog!

Very few black people had any higher education, which was certainly different from Atlanta. I don't remember meeting anyone in my age group who had finished college. But there were at least three or four other black professional people in Lima when Frank and I moved there. There was a dentist, a capable doctor, and a doctor who had problems with alcohol. This second doctor was not very dependable, but he had dependable periods. The Bradfield Community Center was in an old, converted house, which would accommodate maybe twenty people at a time. There was no other community service agency in Lima that accepted blacks. The white organizations did not publicly have in their regulations that no black could use their facilities like they would have in the South. But it was just known. That's why that community center was over *there*—to keep "y'all" from coming over *here*!

Blacks in Lima were divided. You had one group separated from another over on the other side of town. The ones who lived by Lima Locomotive in company housing were the poorer of the two. Those on the opposite side of Bradfield center owned their own homes. That group was the more educated. They had lived in Lima longer, sometimes two generations. They were the ones who would raise money for Bradfield center. They didn't need the kind of support that the newly arrived people did.

The importance of black community centers at the time cannot be emphasized enough. This was where black people went not only for recreation but to get help with their problems. For example, in

Bradfield Community Center, Lima, Ohio, 1938; courtesy of the author.

order to get a job in industry, people coming up from the South needed birth certificates for identification and some form of education and employment history. Usually they had no paperwork at all. They would go to the Bradfield center. Frank would take down their information and write a "To Whom It May Concern" letter substituting for the records these citizens lacked. People called this their "business card," and it was accepted by employers.

Black women needed an outlet. No one ever included them in any of the activities at the local Y. At the Bradfield center, they could take part in athletic leagues, discuss problems their children were having in school, get help in dealing with a landlord. These women ran what we would now call day care for the small children at the center.

I hadn't been in Lima very long when the YWCA asked me to be on its board. I agreed to do it. The Y wouldn't *hire* me as a professional social worker, but it would put me on the board as a volunteer in order to have a black face. I was the first black person, I would guess, to even walk into that Y—certainly the first as a board member. At the Bradfield center I was a volunteer, but pretty soon this had to be limited because I was home with babies.

When Frank and I set up housekeeping in Lima, we lived in an apartment over the office of the dependable doctor, Dr. Dalton. This was in a house near the Bradfield center. We had a bedroom, a kitchen, a bath, and a hall that we made into a second bedroom. Dr. Dalton was on the staff of the major hospital in Lima. That was integrated, which was different from the South. But it was a rare experience for blacks to set foot in that hospital. I can't recall anybody who went. But I'm pretty sure some of Dr. Dalton's patients must have gone there because he was on the staff. And I would have been admitted myself except for what I will relate.

When my mother in Atlanta found out that I was pregnant with my first child, she made up her mind that she would come up to be with me for the delivery. She came and was great. Not only that, but she went down to the center and helped Frank. That's the kind of person she was. But I would not go to the hospital. I did not want any part of that hospital. Dr. Dalton's wife and I were friends, and she had told me some of the horror stories that had come about at this hospital.

These stories were mostly racial. When a black person went there as an emergency, they would say that there were no beds available. But there was something else. When I was pregnant, there were news reports about somebody's baby getting mixed up in Chicago, and they didn't know who it belonged to. My mind ran away with me!

My delivery was right in our apartment over the doctor's office. Dr. Dalton just walked up the steps. It was the talk of the black community. Everybody was trying to determine why it was that Dr. Dalton's patient was not admitted to the hospital. It wasn't that I *wasn't* admitted, but they didn't catch that at first. So Frank Tucker Wood III was born in March 1939 in my own bedroom. He turned out to be almost blond, with blue eyes and light skin. Not very black-looking at all. Everybody said *that's* why you didn't go to the hospital. They would never have let you bring that child home!

By the time I was pregnant with my daughter, Yvonne (or Bonnie, as we called her), we had gotten another place to live in Lima, a lovely big house further away from the center than our apartment. My mother couldn't come for my second delivery. She was ill with cancer and couldn't travel. But she sent word she didn't want me to go to that hospital. So when the time came for the de-

Peggy and Frank III on a trip to Virginia, ca. 1939;
courtesy of the author.

livery, Dr. Dalton drove out to our new house, and Yvonne was born there, in November 1940. What a difference between my daughter and my son! My daughter was brown with dark hair. It was difficult for me and for her as she grew up. People looking at Frank III and Yvonne would say, "Oh Peggy, your little boy is beautiful!" and "Is she your child?"

My husband felt embarrassed by it. The two children would be in the buggy going to town, and you had this little light one and this little dark one. During that period in black experience, you saw much more of that than you do now. All through my family, we have great variety. We have one family where the entire group is light. Every one of them could pass for white. In another family, you have a dark one and a light one. But Frank felt he had to explain it. I'd tell him over and over again, "Don't explain it. He's your child, and she's your child. You accept it. If anybody else doesn't understand it, that is just too bad."

Frank, who loved to garden, dug up the yard at our second house in Lima and planted mustard greens, tomatoes, snaps, and what have you. The garden was essential because the paycheck didn't last for thirty days. Also both of us were very close to our families, and it was part of our routine to go back home in August of each year, the month that Frank had off, two weeks with my parents in Atlanta and two weeks with his in Virginia. We never had enough money to successfully go and act unpoor! So we decided to take fresh vegetables from the garden. The garden was a part of our dignity, I guess you would call it, so that I could say, "Oh, Mom! Look what we've brought." We'd have big bags of snap beans, all strung by me in the Ford as we headed south.

Down the street from us there was an empty lot, and on this lot there were apple trees. Those apples fell on the sidewalk. People

Peggy with Frank III in their garden at Lima, Ohio, ca. 1940; courtesy of the author.

had to walk out on the street to keep from stepping on them. I couldn't wait until those apples began to get ripe. In the early morning, I would take my bag and go down there and get as many apples as I possibly could. I did everything you can do with apples because, the last five days of the month, we would always run out of money.

My unhappiness in Lima, which I have already mentioned, had to do with the town, it is true, but it also had to do with something else. Looking back on it, when I went to Lima I held myself apart from the rest of the black people. I had grown up not in regular communities but in the special, upper-class world of college campuses. In Atlanta my social life revolved around the First Congregational Church, which was also upper class. I arrived in Lima unprepared for the rough and tumble of unsheltered life. (I had certainly never had to pick up apples from the sidewalk before!) People took me for a stuck-up person with her graduate degree coming in to help the downtrodden, and naturally the "downtrodden" were hostile to me.

But I was very fortunate. When she saw how things were going, Mrs. Gamble, Maidie Ruth's mother, befriended me. She helped me see that I would be better off if I related to other women not as the director's wife or as a social worker but as a fellow woman, who had the same problems that they did. (Chief among these problems was that many of us were pregnant or had small children and were watching our non-mother opportunities dwindling to zero.) Before too long, my situation turned around. Young mothers joined me on the front porch where we talked as woman to woman. My next-door neighbor, Mr. Hamilton, the only black policeman in the whole region, was also one of my angels. I would sit in his swing while he tactfully explained to me how the black

Family gathering in Atlanta, early 1940s. From left: Frank III and Peggy Wood, John Wright, Addie Streator Wright, Clarence Wright, Yvonne Wright, and Herbert Wright with his baby and wife; courtesy of the author.

community in Lima worked, both the "up" part of better-off folks and the "down" part.

Mrs. Gamble and Mr. Hamilton saw that I needed help. They made *me* see that I needed help, that I wasn't the caregiver now. This lesson—that I am in the same boat with everyone else—was one of the most valuable in my whole life.

Community centers such as Bradfield were tied into an organization called the National Recreation Association, headquartered in New York. This organization, which started out as the Playground Association of America, had a board of blue bloods dedicated to giving every child in America a chance "to play." The *black* community centers were involved in much more than play. But they did receive financial help from this organization.

The National Recreation Association had a Bureau of Colored Work. Its director was a Mr. E. T. Atwell, who knew my father (the close-knit world of college-educated black people again). Mr. Atwell came to Lima and stayed at our house for months while he helped Frank raise money for Bradfield center. When the fundraising and a building project were completed, Mr. Atwell persuaded Frank that it was time for him to move to on. Mr. Atwell felt that the situation would be better for both Frank and me in Poughkeepsie, New York. With Vassar College there, Frank would be able to get interns to help with activities. And at the larger Poughkeepsie center, I could be hired as a paid member of the staff.

☆
୨

Poughkeepsie

In 1942, after four years in Lima, Frank and I, and little Frank and Yvonne, were off to Poughkeepsie. The United States had just entered World War II. Frank became head of the Catharine Street Community Center, and I was on the staff. Catharine Street had a secretary, but nobody else was paid. All the rest of the large staff were volunteers. The center's board originally wanted to include something for me in Frank's pay. Both of us were against that. I was a trained social worker. If I participated at Catharine Street, I would be doing that for my own wage. The board got the message, and I was paid fifteen hundred dollars. This was about half the salary of the janitor, but at least the principle was established.

My family and I lived on the third floor of the Catharine Street center, which was a narrow, brownstone-type former dwelling. This did not turn out to be such a good idea in that we were on call every minute of the day, including weekends. The coal furnace in the basement had to be stoked, for example. The janitor came early in the morning and did that, but in order for the heat to continue through the day Frank and I had to take turns—which is not how I had imagined things.

The board of directors for the Catharine Street center was about half and half, white and black. We had a close relationship with Vassar College on the edge of Poughkeepsie. Vassar faculty members served on the board. Each year we had about fifteen students who volunteered at the center to help with after-school activities—scout troops, woodworking, or what have you. The Vassar students' backgrounds were basically rich. They were seeing another side of life, but they were great. Frank and I and the kids went to Vassar often in the summer to swim in a lovely lake on campus. We felt entirely welcome there.

Catharine Street was a hub of activity for black people in the Hudson Valley. It was a hub for social service work, for one thing. For example, the Wiltwyck School for boys, an interracial, but heavily black, rehabilitation center supported by Eleanor Roosevelt, would send its large black staff to Catharine Street to take brush-up classes in social work. Catharine Street was also a cultural hub. Well-known actors and singers would come up from New York and perform, often on Sunday afternoon. The Dobbs sisters came, as well as Della Reese before she became famous.

As in Lima, Poughkeepsie's black community contained people who had been there for a long time and those who had just arrived looking for jobs. Many of the older families, which provided the community's leadership, had government employment, particularly at the post office. A letter carrier was looked upon as a leader. I don't believe we had a black teacher when I arrived, but we had two people who were teacher material. One had taught and had been ill or had a family and did not go back to teaching. We had one black policeman. And, of course, we had ministers. But whatever black families were able to achieve would be pushed under the rug. We had some outstanding people, but they were not in high positions. Most were at the level just above the working class. Not a lot of money and no high-sounding title, but they had the influence.

On one side of the Catharine Street center there was an all-black slum, and working-class whites lived on the other. We were on the boundary where blacks and whites were learning to live with one another, not always successfully. While Catharine Street was really a black center, a small percentage of white children did use the facilities. Young husbands, black and white, were now being called up for the Army. Many of the white mothers, like the black ones, had to work to make ends meet. They were desperate for a place to leave their children while they were on the job. Some of these white mothers would leave their preschoolers on the steps of Catharine Street in the morning. The janitor would open up and find them there.

The local grammar school, Samuel F. B. Morse, was a block and a half from the center and also on this borderline between white and black. Morse School was integrated, but not very much. Morse catered mainly to the white families who lived downtown. Black children lived right in the area where Morse was located, and their numbers were expanding, but they generally did not go to Morse. Most of the black children went to a different elementary school quite a ways away. Something must be done, I felt, about this situation. Here was the school halfway between white and black communities. Our community center was also halfway between the two. Yet the school was nearly all white and the center was nearly all black.

Frank III and later Yvonne went to Morse. I never considered sending them across town to the "black" elementary school. Fortunately Frank and I knew enough to demand that our children attend Morse before we even agreed to go to Poughkeepsie. It wasn't because Morse was white. It was because we did not want our children to go to an inferior school. It wouldn't have mattered whether it was 100 percent black or 100 percent white. Some of the parents of the children at the school where it was predominantly black were determined that their children would *not* go to Morse because there were few black children and no black teachers. The parents would say to us, "Why are your children going to Morse? Why didn't you send them here?" We'd tell them, "Because you do not have paper or pencils or books. Wherever we are living—and we pay taxes—our children are going to the best school available."

I don't recall any other black parents in Morse's Parent-Teachers Association. But the PTA was happy to have a black parent willing to participate, and I was willing. The PTA raised money for school activities. There was little emphasis on the community. After my first year in the PTA, I was elected president. I was knowledgeable about the community because I worked at the center. As president, I persuaded the PTA to invite in Morse's black neighbors, who sent their children elsewhere to school, to get to know us. Many came, and the next school year some of them registered their children at Morse. We were leaving token integration behind and beginning real integration.

Now it was true that black students heard nothing about their own history at Morse School. This was typical of the era. With rare exceptions, they would not have heard anything about the black experience anywhere. So some of that we tried to supply at the Catharine Street center.

I mentioned that a few white mothers left their children at the center. All the little ones played together, black and white. They all had tales to tell about what happened at the center when they went home, I'm sure. But I have a hunch that the white children felt a little bit out of it at a black center. Their working-class parents seldom, if ever, came to the center themselves, although some of them lived directly behind it. I suspect they were resentful over

Frank III and Yvonne Wood on Easter Sunday in front of Catharine Street Community Center, Poughkeepsie, New York, ca. 1943; courtesy of the author.

having to have any contact with a black-run organization. My guess is that somebody said to those parents, "You're sending your children to a black community center" or "a nigger community center." They may also have been resentful when they heard that little Frank and Yvonne did well at Morse.

One afternoon, neighborhood white children and my children were out playing in the backyard of the center, a lovely area with a creek running through it. I could watch them from my porch upstairs. That backyard also was behind many of the white people's apartments. A couple of the families over there had never even spoken to any of us. One of these families had two vicious Rottweilers.

That afternoon this family turned the dogs out on my children. The boys from those families ran home as though they knew what was happening. Frank ran away from Yvonne in order to scream to me to come help. The dogs ripped Yvonne's clothes off. They slashed her leg. We took Yvonne right away to the hospital where she had stitches, and she recovered. But it was awful, not only the devastation to my child, but also what it represented. This attack had to have been planned. More than one family was involved, and it had to be at a time when the center was not in business and few people were around. The dog owners knew that. There was a hatred. They were looking for a way to get back at us. I don't think a black family would have turned dogs on a white child. All the months that we had worked with these kids seemed to go for nothing. All our efforts to bridge the gap between white and black seemed to go down the drain.

In Poughkeepsie we could never have had the Rottweilers' owners put in jail. In any court case that we made of it, they would have found some way to make it our own fault. But mainly we didn't want this to become a racial conflict that caused violence in the community. That would have destroyed whatever small relationship there was between the white families at one end of the street and the black families at the other. So we used it as a teaching experience. The churches got involved. We had meetings. But this "teaching experience," I'll have to admit, was one-sided because very few whites chose to participate.

The doctor who patched up Yvonne told us to get a dog right away or the incident would haunt her for the rest of her life. He gave us the name of a family that raised English shepherds, which are faithful and calm. So we went to get a dog. The two kids picked a puppy out of a litter of ten. That was Billy. Billy was with them until they went to college. He became an honorary member of the Catharine Street staff and protected the children. Billy walked them each day to Morse School and back.

In the 1940s, things were beginning to boil up from down under in the black community. Changes were about to be made, and everyone sensed it. They were about to be made in the school system. They were about to be made in employment. Some black women were now working in sales at department stores that, incidentally, wouldn't serve them if they came in as customers. But when we arrived the city of Poughkeepsie was not in the lead. It wasn't ready to move on integration unless it felt pressure. It was content with keeping the races pretty much apart.

In Poughkeepsie I was able to take an aggressive position without this touching Frank too much. He was off on the sidelines viewing the situation. *I'm* the one who stirred things up. That was the relationship that we fell into. It had to be this way. If Frank got too far out front, he would have risked losing the Community Chest money essential to the Catharine Street center's existence.

Frank was very effective, though, in his own way, working around discrimination and patiently undermining it, rather than hitting it head on.

These were practical considerations. I could raise my voice; he couldn't. But we were also temperamentally different. Frank could close his eyes to unacceptable things and quietly get over them for the sake of the center. I was not willing to do that. Frank had come up in a different world than I had. His whole childhood and young adulthood had been a definite segregation program, where he *felt* the segregation every day. He had to move out of his community to get an education. His expectations were lower. To him, the very fact that we had mixed board meetings at Catharine Street was a step up. I, on the other hand, had grown up expecting to be the equal of anybody else who came along. I could not sit still and watch this person treated one way and that person treated another.

This was a time of uncertainty. Light-skinned Latinos were migrating into the Hudson Valley to work on the farms. Who was to serve them—the Catharine Street center or the community center across town for whites? Who was to guide the black teenagers, particularly the boys, now that so many fathers were off in the Army? How would the men react to what they found in the military? And how would this affect the community when they came home?

There was much excitement in the black community in 1942 as men were called up. Men would bring their notices to the center, and everybody would be talking about them. "What day is it?" and "What are you going to do?" and "Who's going to be in charge of your children and your family?" The men had high hopes when they went in. But they came back upset at how they were treated.

Even those with a good education were segregated to lowly jobs. Several of the young black men from Poughkeepsie had been postal workers before they went and had college backgrounds. But they didn't get anything on *that* level in the Army. They expressed their frustration quite a bit, but, at the same time, they did not want to be seen as complaining in wartime. Also they were concerned that if they did too much complaining, they might not be offered their old civilian jobs when they came home.

Almost every one of the young men who came to the Catharine Street center were called up. Frank was not, which really upset him. They could just as well have taken a pistol and shot him. He had the same enthusiasm as these other guys. He felt that he could not face the men who had young children just like ours and explain why he was not called up. He actually had a breakdown. But he was viewed as too important to the community. No matter how much he objected, his wartime role was to be at the center.

In this time of change, as I said, I was the one to stir things up. It seemed to come naturally. One example was the church. When we first went to Poughkeepsie, Frank took our children to Sunday school at a black Baptist church. Frank's tradition was Baptist, and this also put him with many of the people who used the center. But after a while, I took little Frank and Yvonne to the white Congregational Church in Poughkeepsie. They disliked the Baptist church, not, of course, because it was black. Little Frank and Yvonne didn't like it because, as the children of the director of Catharine Street, they were on center stage all the time. If they made the slightest mistake, it made the rounds in the community. They didn't want to be on display, to always be upholding the name of the director.

Our going to the Congregational church, which was much

nearer to the center than the Baptist, had nothing to do with whether the church was white or black. Frank III and Yvonne liked it because children they knew at Morse School went there. I'll have to add that it was the denomination that had played such an important part in the Wright family's life, and it appealed to me for that reason. We were warmly received at the Congregational church. Naturally, the minister knew my father. But we were the only black people in the church.

This wasn't easy, either for me or for Frank, who remained at the Baptist church. People couldn't understand why the director's wife and his children would leave a black church and go to a white church. But the welfare of my children, as I saw it, came ahead of other considerations.

Another time people got upset was over a basketball game. The Catharine Street center had a team of teenage boys. They were big and they were good. The fathers coached and refereed at the games. But now the war was on, and many fathers had been inducted into the service. Frank and I wanted to make sure that we could continue our work with their sons. One time Catharine Street was scheduled to play a black public school in New York City. Our reputation had preceded us, and excitement was high. We went down from Poughkeepsie by train. The boys were there, the crowd was there, but no referee and no coach for the other side. I became the referee as well as the coach for both teams. I had to do it all. Somehow we got through the game. Afterwards people were happy that I had been able to go out there and keep down any fights.

But when we got back to Poughkeepsie, the word went out. "Oh, did you know Mrs. Wood acted as a referee?" It didn't sit well with the center's board. The board felt that it was beneath the dig-

Peggy, Yvonne, and Frank III on a ferry in Virginia,
1940s; courtesy of the author.

nity of the director's wife to have refereed a game. Later, when Dunbar Center in Syracuse, New York, was interviewing Frank for a job, it sent someone down to Poughkeepsie. The Catharine Street board talked about what a wonderful person Frank was, but don't fool with his wife!

I was an irritant to the Catharine Street board in other ways. The board was concerned that programs help the black children who lived in the neighborhood down below the center. To the board, that meant primarily sports. Nothing else was important. But a purely athletic program was too limited for the children. The children needed to discover what their gifts were, which might not be on the basketball court. I taught athletics, but that did not satisfy me because I knew that the boys were getting much more out of it than the girls.

I knew modern dance. I told the girls the story of Martha Graham, how she had come to Tuskegee and Talladega, and why it meant so much to me. I decided that I was going to teach the girls in the center modern dance. I got a phonograph and records. One day a week we were doing modern dance from Martha Graham. It took quite a while to learn this step and understand why you did the other, but the girls did master it, and they were enthusiastic. I was not just the teacher. I was also the learner. We were all doing this together.

The board met right above the room where I taught dance. One day some members on the board said, "Why is that music in the center? Why do we hear that music?" Frank proudly said, "Oh, didn't you know? Peg is teaching modern dancing." "Oh no! No!" Unfortunately, there were the two black women on the board who were active in the Baptist church, which frowned on dancing. To them the thought of teaching dance was scandalous. Somebody on the board said, "But you haven't seen the worst of it. *She* is on the floor!"

The board decided to take a look. They came down the steps from upstairs, swung open the door, and the woman who was so against it was in the front. This helped me because I knew then why they were there. But we never stopped. The music was on. The woman pointed, "There she is!"

I was down on the floor, and I waved. I knew what was coming because Frank had told me about rumblings on the board. I think the name "modern dance" was more than they could take. There I was on the floor with my little skinny skirt. One of the people on the board who was most against this was a black dentist, who was one of the few professionals in the black community. We continued. They went back upstairs and had a tumultuous meeting. Some wanted to kick me off the staff altogether, and the others raised Cain about that. But I weathered the storm, and dance became one of the most requested programs that we had. People would say, "Oh Mrs. Wood, would you come to our meeting and explain to us about Martha Graham's modern dancing." They even wanted me to demonstrate steps and play the music. I would take one or two of our girls.

All of this swimming against the tide took its toll. When Frank was courted by the center in Syracuse, I was happy about the development. My main motivation was to get away! I wanted to get us out of the apartment above the center where we were never off duty. I, for one, needed to be off duty. My doctor said, "You've had it."

Peggy and Frank Wood and Poughkeepsie's Catharine Street Community Center

Charles L. James, professor of English, Swarthmore College

I was born in Poughkeepsie in 1934 and began using the Catharine Street Community Center when I was eight or nine years old. My earliest memory of the center is associated with Peggy and Frank Wood.

IBM had not yet come to this region in the early 1940s, but two important industries within the city did employ a sizeable number of workers. One was the DeLaval Separator Company, which made dairy machinery for milking cows and separating the cream. When this factory converted to war work, it took on local black laborers, including my father. The other industry was the Schatz Federal Bearing Corporation, a ball bearing manufacturer whose business boomed during the war. Schatz attracted industrial workers, both white and black, from far and wide. Many of the black employees and their families gravitated to Catharine Street Community Center.

During World War II, what had been a trickle of black immigrants to Poughkeepsie grew to a stream, drawn by the prospect of farm work in the Hudson Valley. A shortage of laborers created by the war led farmers to hire black seasonal workers from the South. They were transported by truck to harvest crops in the surrounding countryside: apples, currants, cherries, beans, peaches, pears, grapes. They would seek relaxation in the towns nearby, including Poughkeepsie. Some simply decided to stay on when the trucks left. Many ended up living in neighborhoods adjacent to the Catharine Street center.

Yet in the 1940s, the area around the center was by no means all black. Many families of immigrant whites—Greeks, Italians, Irish—also lived there and sent their children to Samuel F. B. Morse School, where

Peggy Wood's children were students. Some few of these white immigrant families came to the center. However, I have no recollection of any of them playing on sports teams, and though a few preteens would show up for after-school activities, those connections inevitably broke off over time.

At Christmas there would be large gatherings of the neighborhood children at the Catharine Street center. An enormous Christmas tree sat in the main room where dances and large events otherwise were held. Frank would dress in the full Santa Claus outfit, and Peggy would be Mrs. Santa Claus. Packages, beautifully wrapped, would appear, with each of our names handwritten on a label. Peggy and Frank would call our names and invite each child to come forward to receive a package and a stocking full of candy.

The center had after-school programs for both boys and girls, with Frank handling the boys and Peggy the girls. We boys would do woodwork projects and play games. Ping-pong and pool were both popular, but especially ping-pong. Frank Wood was as avid a ping-pong competitor as he was a tennis player. Meanwhile, Peggy led the girls in other activities.

These included scouting programs, from Brownies through Girl Scouts. But Peggy also introduced programs that were more modern than some folks were comfortable with. Modern dancing was one of them. She had a very strong interest in dance, and she organized a class of preteen and teenage girls that she taught with great energy. This meant dressing to suit the occasion, in tights or shorts or both. It also meant lying on the floor and practicing synchronized routines. We guys were amused and attracted by some of this stuff. But Peggy was dedicated to it and that was that.

To me, Peggy was a model of female decorum that really had an impact on me. She was competitive and energetic but never lacking in *decorum, always displaying good taste in her manner and speech. She expected no less from us. When we boys walked into the center, we were expected to remove our hats out of respect. I remember Peggy Wood "enforcing" that practice, usually by no more than a raised eyebrow. We kids had enough regard for her to feel that we should be on our best behavior in her presence. She was a highly principled person who earned our respect and took no nonsense.*

Catharine Street center was a key social site, especially for us kids. The only other institution that came anywhere near the center's attraction for blacks on the north side of town was the church. Catharine Street center was the focal point on weekdays and sometimes on Saturdays; church was Sundays. There was such a range of daily events going on at the center that the building would be busy until about 10:00 P.M. What with the organized sports teams, the scout troops, and the directed after-school activities, there always seemed to be a bustle. The teenage Friday night dance attracted black kids from downtown and out of town. Bottom line: it was where colored kids went to socialize.

When I was a Catharine Street member, the only other place where we could go for recreation was the YMCA. But that was only available at a single, designated time each week: Tuesday night, 7:00 to 10:00. And it was strictly for males. I vividly recollect that Tuesday night was called Torch Club Night, when the YMCA gymnasium and the swimming pool were available to black kids—colored kids.

For me, the Wood family could be considered a modern standard in the midst of Poughkeepsie's ethnicity. They were a progressive, forward-looking family of young Americans on the move, full of vitality, ambition, and self-assurance. They were a model American family with a son and a daughter and a dog named Billy, not Spot. They were devout, I believe. They were patriotic (the flag flew faithfully at Catharine Street center, and we saluted it at certain events, especially events related to Boy Scouts and Girl Scouts). They were athletic and outdoorsy. They even drove the "American automobile," a Ford. Today, I think of them as unselfconscious paradigms of the modern era, one generation beyond the black middle-class mind-set of "established" Poughkeepsie.

By this I mean that Peggy and Frank seemed at the time to be far less conservative than their local counterparts in Poughkeepsie. When I speak of the black middle-class mind-set, I mean the conservative postures of Poughkeepsie's professional black families and of the older black families whose Hudson Valley ancestry preceded the Civil War. Some of these folk had the ear of the local white bankers, ministers, fund-raisers, and entrepreneurs throughout the valley. Their notions of decorum were as staunch and inflexible as those of their most respected Southside white professional counterparts, if not more. They worried about scandal, but they also worried deeply (and widely within the race, as the expression goes) about untoward appearances—bad behavior that reflected on the race.

I think Peggy and Frank brought a more cosmopolitan view of life to the more insular dark citizenry of the region. They represented positive family life values, but they were also comparative youngsters whose values were a bit too modern to suit some of the folks "in charge" at this time. I think this is the reason many young families admired them and why they were a breath of fresh air to the local teenagers.

PART THREE

Civil Rights, Human Rights

※

Syracuse in the 1950s

My family and I moved to Syracuse in 1950. Frank came ahead, and I stayed behind in Poughkeepsie for several months to supervise Catharine Street Community Center on an interim basis. Dunbar Center in Syracuse, which had hired Frank as its director, was similar to Catharine Street. Black people had the same kind of problems and needs everywhere. But change was in the air in Syracuse, as it had been in Poughkeepsie. This was just when the movement for civil rights was gaining momentum all over the United States.

Dunbar's board members wanted to avoid bringing someone to Syracuse who was an activist. They liked the fact that Frank had kept down violence in Poughkeepsie, that he had been a calming influence. But they worried that I was more of an activist than he was. So they let it be known from the beginning that they did not want me on the staff. This was fine with me because the pressure had been overwhelming at Catharine Street toward the end.

When Dunbar Center offered Frank the director's job, Frank said that he would only accept it if the board helped us buy a home. We were not going to live over the center again. The Dunbar board agreed and assigned one of its members, a white lawyer, to work this out. The places this lawyer found for us to live were within two or three blocks of Dunbar, which was then located on South Townsend Street. Dunbar was on one side of the street, and the Pioneer Homes public housing project was on the other.

The lawyer only looked within about three blocks of Dunbar Center. He picked out a house on McBride. It was a house on a corner with no yard. The windows were broken out of it. He said to Frank that he'd found this beautiful house that would be fine because we had the two children. He wanted us to come up to see it. He explained that it was in a black neighborhood, which was not anything that would bother us, of course.

When I got to Syracuse with the children and the dog, the lawyer took us to see this house. I saw it sitting there with no yard and windows broken out, and I said, "Where will the children play?" The lawyer said, "Play?" I said, "Yes." He said, "They have the center." I said, "Where would they play at the house?" He said, "Come out here and I'll show you. You see that building right down there?" He said, "That's the movie house for the black people." And he said, "Most people send their children there in the afternoon, and they can see the movies." He was a member of the Dunbar board! Frank and I were so upset. Frank said right away that he would not take the job as long as that man was involved in finding us a house.

At that point, another lawyer on the Dunbar board stepped forward. This was Benjamin Shove of the law firm then called Hancock, Dorr, Ryan, and Shove. He had a fit when he heard about how the first lawyer had treated us. Ben Shove said to Frank, "You find a home. Wherever it is, I'll give you the money for the mortgage." And that's what happened. We found a nice home on Fine View Place, below where the Carrier Dome is now.

In the early 1950s, there were attractive homes on Fine View

Place. There was no elevated highway running through there then, but there were railroad tracks. It could not have been better for my son because he loved trains. He and his friends were able to see every train that passed by. Fine View was white in the early 1950s. It was in Croton School's district. Had we lived anywhere else in the city Frank III and Yvonne would have had to go to Madison School, and that would have caused a problem, as I will explain.

The Dunbar board was about 75 percent white and 25 percent black when Frank arrived. Dunbar had an organization called the Friends of Dunbar that met at the First Baptist Church downtown. The Friends of Dunbar were, I think, all white. The Dunbar board may not have wanted too much activism, but it did not object when Frank quietly expanded the scope of the center.

Frank conducted political education classes at Dunbar, particularly focused on voting. Not to sign up people for the Republicans or Democrats, but to get across the idea that this was a way to address segregation in employment and housing and all the other problems of discrimination. Parents of children in Dunbar's nursery school came to these sessions. The men had not been able to get a decent job in industry, and the women simply had not voted before. A lot of them had never belonged to any kind of community group. This was a learning process. How do you function in community groups? What do you do when you encounter somebody you're not in agreement with?

Another of Frank's efforts to address problems in the community involved beauty parlors. The many beauty parlors in Syracuse were supposed to be inspected by the state. Most were run from somebody's kitchen and were not really authorized. But nobody ever went to inspect them. They started in the morning and ended at night, and it was just one head after another, clipping and straightening. Cleanliness was not always taken into consideration. The floors needed to be swept after so many customers, and this was not done. People would come to Frank and say, "Mr. Wood, I went to so-and-so's shop"—that would be the kitchen—"and I had to sit there all day long with my kids." And they would say, "I shouldn't have to do that. We should be able to make an appointment just like anybody else." One person had a beauty parlor, and the black women used to complain that you could not make an appointment. They would call her and say, "I'd like to come in at three o'clock because my kids get home from school then, and I can take them." But she would not have put on the books who she was having at three, so this person might have to wait until five o'clock with her children. Frank met with beauty parlor operators to talk about what would be expected of them if an inspector *did* come. Also how to schedule patrons to minimize the waiting.

But this is looking ahead. In 1950 we arrived in Syracuse. Frank went to work at Dunbar, and I bided my time at Fine View Place. I needed a break. The doctor back in Poughkeepsie had said to me, "Don't rush, rock on the porch, and go slow for a while." I had several requests for interviews from people who knew that I had graduated from the School of Social Work. By the end of the year, I thought the time had come to take a job.

A Captain E. M. Brewer from the Salvation Army visited me and described his organization's new Family and Personal Services Department. Captain Brewer was not happy with it. I thought this is where I'd like to go, to a program that was just beginning. Nowhere in our discussion did anything come up about the horrors of race relations in the community or the fact that blacks were restricted to one area of town. He talked about *people* and what an agency like the Salvation Army could do. But the important thing, it seemed to me at the time, was that Captain Brewer recognized that the Salvation Army was not meeting the needs of poor people, white and black, in Syracuse.

I agreed to head the Salvation Army's family services department, the first person with a social work degree hired locally. So far as I know, I was the first black person hired, as well. My pay was $2,800 per year for a full-time job. Captain Brewer wrote me that "the full responsibility of our welfare program will rest on your shoulders." He also wrote that "you will be expected to uphold at all times, the high and holy principles that have undergirded the work of the Salvation Army since its inception in 1865 by William Booth."

The Salvation Army, both nationally and in Syracuse, was overwhelmingly white with little feel for the black community. When I got there, it had probably the least in the way of an outreach program to black people of any social service agency in the city. Captain Brewer was headed in the right direction, but he was not the Salvation Army. The organization itself was slow to recognize the needs of blacks and not about to change very quickly. As a part of my *being*, my first interest was in the black community. So here we had the seeds of trouble.

When I went to work as the family services director, the Salvation Army was located in a block of East Genesee Street that no longer exists, between Montgomery and State, not far from the old Yates Hotel. There were vacant lots in the vicinity, and that's where crime took place. Homeless people and drunks hung out in the bars, sleeping on benches or in the weeds or under elevated railroad tracks a short distance away.

The family services department was on the second floor, and the Salvation Army chapel was on the first floor. I saw clients either downstairs in the entrance to the chapel or upstairs when they were sober enough to make it to the second floor. My caseload consisted of transients and homeless people.

The transients were usually men who came to Syracuse by the railroad or by hitchhiking and remained here for a short period. Some came as migrant workers in the summer to pick crops and stayed on for a short period of time. Many were from the West. When they got laid off, they hopped on a boxcar until they could find another job. The transients were mainly white. Black men did not ride the rails so much. The Salvation Army claimed that it turned no one away, but it really didn't want these men to settle down in Syracuse. The goal with the transients was to send them on their way.

The homeless were different. They were local people who were seriously down on their luck and often alcoholic. We needed to get these folks off the street, particularly in winter. I sent them—as well as transients—either to the Workman's Hotel or to a rooming house called the Jackson where they could flop at fifty cents a night. The Workman's Hotel was located on West Fayette Street near West Street. The Jackson was located on Almond Street near East Washington, and it was very run down. My idea was to renovate the Jackson Hotel so that it could be another Workman's Hotel. But this was totally thrown out when urban renewal came along. I also sent people to the movies to warm up.

The other solution for hardcore homeless people was to pack them off to the penitentiary. Many of them knew the system. If they got drunk enough or loitered enough, they would be sent to the penitentiary in Jamesville, just outside of town, for anywhere from one to six months. At Jamesville the homeless would be warm and well fed and away from alcohol. When these people were about to come out of the pen, the police would call me, and then I would look out for them as best I could.

In addition to the men, I had quite a list of homeless women. They also lacked a job until something came here like the state fair that provided extra employment. Many of these women existed off of prostitution. You had to deal with both the prostitution and the hunger. They were my *night* customers. That's when they came to me for help. I had two particular women on my list for years and years. I always tried to get them in jail in cold months where they would be cared for.

As strange as it may seem, one of the most helpful people to me in my Salvation Army years was the bartender at a tavern near my office. Some of the homeless men went directly to this bartender when they got their welfare checks. He handed out the money to them gradually so that they would not spend it all at once or have somebody steal it from them. The bartender was also helpful with one of my longtime clients, an alcoholic man I'll call "John," who was about fifty years old. John's parents, who lived in the suburbs, would send a check to the bar each month. The bartender would dole out enough money for John to have food, but, as the end of the month approached, the money would run out. When that happened, John would come and sit by my desk, often as drunk as could be. "I need help. I can't go any further," he would say. Sometimes I would give John scripts for meals. Other times, particularly if cold weather was coming on, I would call the police and say, "It's time to arrest him."

The Salvation Army had a camp on Lake Ontario, run by Captain Brewer and staffed largely by college students. It was excellent. I did all of the evaluations for who should go to camp. The camp in no way discriminated against black children. And the photograph in the newspaper of the annual Thanksgiving dinner would show a black face or two, surrounded by the ladies in furs who gave money, usually for building improvements. But that was about as far as the interracial part went. I had a hard time dealing with this. Locally and nationally the Salvation Army was consumed with having magnificent physical plants, particularly their chapels, and not consumed with solving inner-city problems. The Army spent liberally for beautiful apartments, used as stopping places for its officers who came here to meetings. But it neglected programs to help the poor, particularly the black poor. That's one thing that worries me about faith-based social service programming today.

My caseload of homeless people was mostly white because the Salvation Army did not make any special effort to bring blacks in. Salvation Army congregations throughout the United States were almost totally white. Many of the officers themselves had been in a transient or homeless situation. The Army didn't foresee success for a black. "It'll be a waste of time if we were to treat him right," seemed to be the attitude. It was ingrained. The Army was like a Catholic organization expecting you to respond to the needs of Catholics first, regardless of what your thoughts were. I couldn't quite do that.

There was one time I really made a fuss. One of my duties at the Salvation Army was to refer pregnant teenagers to maternity homes. They were white, sometimes fairly well off, but a bit foolish. These girls and their parents used our services at the Salvation Army. The girls would leave Syracuse and usually go to the Salvation Army's maternity home in Buffalo. They "went on a trip" until the baby was born, had the baby put up for adoption, and came back home, with no one supposedly the wiser.

But the same benefits were denied black girls. The attitude was that they usually just have their babies at home, and the grandmother takes care of them. I could not get a pregnant black girl into a Salvation Army maternity home. I simply could not swallow that. It was extremely difficult for me to accept the role of favoring people of one color and discriminating against people of another. I finally decided that something must be done. I decided that a crusade was needed.

A name was given to me of a young lady who was pregnant and black. I decided that I would make a referral to the Salvation Army's maternity home in Buffalo for her. That would have been, as far as our agency was concerned, the first black person referred to the home. She had attempted to get in the Episcopal maternity home in Utica without success. That was the first one, and it caused quite a bit of upset. The Syracuse Salvation Army officials felt that I should not be fighting the Buffalo home.

But, nevertheless, this young lady got in, and her stay was paid for by welfare here in Syracuse. But she did not follow the usual procedure of having the baby put up for adoption. This was crucial. The expectant mother normally decided before she ever left for the home that she would give the baby up for adoption. This particular young lady did not want that. She wanted to bring the baby back home. That helped to get her in because the white maternity home knew nothing about adoption for black children.

In New York State, white agencies did not become involved in an adoption for a black child. If you were white, you could not ask for a black child. A black child had to go to a black family, and, if that family happened to be light, they would not allow a dark child to go with them. Also black people didn't want black mothers in white maternity homes any more than the agencies did.

They didn't want anybody meddling with their children. As a result of all of this, we had an army of black children waiting for adoption in New York.

A local Presbyterian minister was our next-door neighbor when we lived on Fine View Place. He and his wife were white. They had one child and wanted to adopt a second. The minister and his wife decided that they wanted to adopt a black child. They went to the Child and Family Service Agency and did everything they possibly could to adopt a black child. But the agency told them that it would never be responsible for a black child growing up alongside a white child in Syracuse. And the couple did not succeed in adopting a nonwhite child. That's the way things worked in the 1950s.

Fine View Place suited Frank and me when we were raising our family. We both had the absorbing roles in the community that I have described. But we also found time to be a normal family. Maybe not too normal. One time we bought a box of chickens—one rooster, a hen, and several chicks. We had them down in the basement. The idea was that when we went to Virginia for a homecoming, we would take these chickens to help feed Frank's big family. These chicks kept growing bigger and bigger. We had to bring them up from the basement and put them on the first floor. We had a little trailer in back of our car. Along with the food from the garden, we tucked in the chickens when we drove south. Of course, Frank's father and mother had loads of chickens, so this was just a drop in the bucket. But to us, it was doing our part.

In 1965, Syracuse University bought our house and tore it down. We moved to Albert Road off East Genesee Street at the eastern edge of Syracuse. This was a white, almost suburban neighborhood, much further from the core of the city than Fine

View Place. We were again accepted without any trouble. Professional people and people connected with LeMoyne College lived there, which certainly helped.

But we raised our family on Fine View, as I mentioned earlier, in the Croton Elementary School district. Croton School, now Dr. King Magnet School, was only two blocks from our house. It was nearly all white when we moved to Syracuse, catering to many of the children of Syracuse University faculty. Black children went to the elementary and junior high schools set aside for them—to Washington Irving School on Madison Street and then to Madison School, also on Madison Street. If they didn't drop out—and many did—they went on to Central High School downtown with white students. At Central, there was a fork in the road between the academic side of the school and the trades side. The number of black teenagers who got past this fork into the academic side was not very large.

Frank III went to Croton for one year, then moved up, not to predominantly black Madison School, but to Theodore Roosevelt on Brighton Avenue, which he attended with only a handful of other black children. Yvonne went the same route. Frank was elected president of the student council at Roosevelt and made top grades. He already thought of becoming an engineer. But when he went on to Central High School, he, and his father and I, were in for an unpleasant surprise.

Frank III was excellent in math. But when he entered the academic side of Central High in 1953, he was told that he could not be enrolled in the first math course in the normal sequence leading to college. Frank kept coming home and saying to us that he could not get in the math class. My husband and I went to Central and asked the assistant principal why our son had not been able to get in the class. I can see it now. The assistant principal sat there wringing his hands. He said there was no more room in the class. I said, "What about the other children in the class, how did they get enrolled?" "Oh, they passed the examination," he said. I said, "What examination?" He said, "They were given an exam to get in their class." I said, "You left my child out of the exam and he is an A student in math. He is going to college in engineering and he needs to have this math course!" More hand-wringing. I seldom saw my husband lose his cool, but this time he did.

We could not get our child in the math sequence for college, which is what often happened to black people. The assistant principal even sat there and said that our son's teacher at Theodore Roosevelt had said that he would make an excellent trombone player! The only way that Frank was able to keep on track for college was to wait until the end of that year and take an examination. He passed the exam, of course, and then was admitted to the math class. My husband and I were ready to burn the school down!

This is what happened to black young people in the 1950s in Syracuse. We lost many of our older teenagers at Central. Many got discouraged and dropped out. It came from exactly what I described. When they arrived, no matter what their background was, no matter who their parents were, they were sent into the noncollege stream. Unless you found it out right away, it would be too late. And, by the way, the trombone player later got a full scholarship in chemical engineering to Bucknell University. His sister graduated from the University of Michigan and then took a Ph.D. from the Maxwell School at Syracuse University.

I'll give another example of what went on. Yvonne and Marcia Foster were like sisters. They went to Central together. Yvonne and Marcia always got very low grades in one particular class, where they were the only black students. The school had an open house. Marcia's mother could not go, even though she was as angry as I was. She did not want to do anything that would jeopardize Marcia's relationship with the school. That's the way most parents felt. But I went to the school. The teacher was standing by the classroom door smiling as the parents came in. I think it was a writing class. My daughter was always good in writing. The teacher had the students' work on their desks. I told her I was Yvonne's mother and that I was there for Marcia as well. The teacher responded as though she didn't know who I was talking about. So I said, "May I see her desk?" I went back, and there was nothing on Yvonne's desk, no papers or anything else that the other students had. I asked the teacher if she would please close the door to the room and talk to me privately. I said, "You shut this door because I want to talk to you, and I don't want anybody in the hall to hear me." I said, "You have cut my daughter out of everything that she might have wanted in the future. You have done it on purpose, and you've done it to only two people in your class." I said now, "Would you explain to me why you did it?"

The teacher said, "Oh, Mrs. Wood"—tears running down her face—"I hope you don't stand in my way of getting my retirement because I'm leaving this year. I can't take any more of this." I said, "Don't worry about it." I said, "You've already lost it as far as I'm concerned. But I want to know what you have done to my daughter." She said to me, "I know all of the children and their parents. I have met with them from time to time. I don't know you." I said, "You mean to tell me that you marked my child's papers down because you didn't know me?" I might say that I was pretty ugly, and I had to leave. But she left that classroom crying, saying, "All I have done for these children at Central, and this is the kind of treatment that I get." But that's what had been happening to the black children. By the time they got through with a teacher like this and got shunted to one side in the streaming program, they never went back.

If the school system tended to keep the races apart, housing patterns did the same. Frank and I lived in white neighborhoods, but the overwhelming majority of black people did not. Most blacks were congregated in the center of Syracuse in the city's Fifteenth Ward. In the 1950s, the Fifteenth Ward was roughly bordered by Erie Boulevard to the north, Burt Street to the south, University Avenue to the east, and Montgomery Street to the west. But the ward was irregular, bulging out to the east beyond University Avenue to include Ashworth Place, for example. Ashworth was where black people who had good jobs and owned their own homes lived. This was the upper crust.

Below the Fifteenth Ward, at about Castle and Kennedy Streets, the neighborhood, which is black today, turned white. Longtime residents still lived in their big houses, which had not yet been cut up into apartments. Danforth Congregational Church (whose building now houses the New Jerusalem Church of God in Christ) was just below Kennedy on South Salina Street, and wealthy white professional people lived in the area around it. (I'll come back to why I recall this so clearly.) But the Fifteenth Ward was where most of the black people lived. I would estimate that in 1950 that meant five thousand people, but this number was beginning to expand rapidly.

For as long as anybody could remember, black laborers had migrated seasonally up the East Coast from the South to work the farms in the Northeast, including upstate New York. Very seldom did you get lone men coming up the migrant trail. It was generally families, and they came as a part of a team, often on a bus. The family hoed or picked crops and maybe ended up near Syracuse when it got cold. They drifted into town, got on relief for a time, and their children went to the public schools. In the mid- to late fifties, that started to change as big farm and orchard owners began to fly in workers from Puerto Rico, almost all of them males. This meant that many of the traditional migrants arrived here and found no work. Some of these, like the more successful migrants earlier, settled down in Syracuse.

The children of the migrants grew up to take service or menial employment. Many of the women ended up as maids or cooks for white people, and many of the men were kept down in jobs at the manual labor level. Here is where you saw the effects of discrimination. Sometimes a mother who had a household job would be forced to find a theater where her child could see the movie and stay until she finished work. And many of the men just gave up trying to move up the ladder in an occupation.

Farm migration didn't account for all of Syracuse's black population by any means. Some people had come because they knew somebody here or for a wide variety of other reasons. And an important percentage—I would estimate 10 percent—were descended from former slaves who came up on the Underground Railroad before the Civil War. They remained up here and had children. Their descendants in many cases became leaders in the Syracuse black community. These folks showed very little of an I'm-better-than-you attitude toward the newer arrivals. Everybody lived together in the Fifteenth Ward. The churches had a variety of members.

So much for how people got here. My lasting regret was to watch them leave. Decent employment for blacks was so scarce here that many bright young people left at the first opportunity. Some went to New York City. Some went back to the South. Some of them went to Rochester or Buffalo where there were more jobs. This was a loss to the community.

The Fifteenth Ward was described in the Syracuse newspapers as if it were one big slum or a "tenderloin." That was not true. You had the high and the low. Life went on in its entirety—the good and the bad. You had people who had a wonderful background, who could keep up their property and send their children to college. Down the street, there might be people living in dire poverty. Because we didn't have drugs on a large scale, crime was not a big problem. Kids used to walk home from Dunbar Center at night without any problem. Poverty was a problem. Tuberculosis was. Polio was. All of those things had more negative impact than crime.

There were many churches in the Fifteenth Ward—from the mainline Baptist and Methodist ones to the House of the Golden Slippers type. It was common to see ministers sitting in front of their churches on stools. They would be out in the neighborhood so that, if any drunks bothered children going to and from school, something could be done about it. They saw any mischief that was going on near the church and stopped it. If children were doing something they shouldn't, their parents would hear about it. The preachers didn't have a job particularly. They got their money from parishioners so they could afford to sit outside, and this was great for the community.

Most of the corner stores in the Fifteenth Ward were owned by whites. Black people without cars couldn't get to the A&P and had to trade at these little stores. There was one of them next door to Dunbar Center. Frank did all of the grocery shopping for our family—I am not a food person!—and that is where he went a lot of the time.

Frank and I had a social life, of course, in the few hours that we were off duty. One of our outlets was the Chez Nous Club, which met once a month in a member's home. This club was for black professional people. Its membership, mostly couples, included Dr. Abbie Washington, one of two black doctors in Syracuse, Marjorie Carter, the first black school teacher in Syracuse I believe, and Harriet Fields, the wife of an engineer at General Electric. Evelyn Washington, Rena Hawkins, and I formed the club for two reasons. Black professionals needed a way to socialize together, and we wanted to provide outlets for our children. We would also welcome visiting black professors who came to Syracuse University. Word spread about Chez Nous, and we eventually had members as far away as Schenectady and Binghamton.

Chez Nous met on Saturday nights for a good meal and conversation. We would talk about plays we had seen or trips we had taken. All of us were travelers, so there were lots of outings to describe. In the summer, we met sometimes at Green Lakes Park. The husbands would play golf, and the wives would talk among themselves in one of the shelters by a barbeque pit. As the years went by, we were looking for ways that our children could socialize at the dating age.

Chez Nous sponsored a debutante ball each year starting in the mid-fifties. It was held at first on the second floor of the Harrison Bakery, which was then on Harrison Street near McBride. In later years, we shifted to a building on West Genesee Street just off Clinton Square across from the old post office. We always had a black band, usually of the pick-up variety, but very good. Beforehand we trained the boys and girls, but particularly the boys, as to what they were expected to do at a debutante ball (although it didn't always turn out exactly as we had planned). Our boys would rent tuxedos, and our girls would be beautifully gowned. The boys bought the girls corsages and brought them to the dance, usually in the back seat of the parents' car.

Chez Nous was social. But Frank and I met other people in Syracuse who were more political and more radical. Communism was not by any means a dead letter in the black community in the 1950s. The Communists talked the talk and walked the walk. They did not try to hide their convictions. They saw the problems in the black community, and they went out there and tried to solve them. Here in Syracuse individuals would have get-togethers in their homes, and you were invited and you went. The idea, I thought, was to come out of a meeting with something positive, not worrying too much about whether some of the people leaned toward the Communists. That's a dangerous position to be in. You wanted to be a part of solving problems, but you couldn't do that effectively by being tied to the people who were doing the underground work.

Many of our friends and acquaintances were sitting on the fence. I believe there may have been some few who were actually card-carrying members of the Communist Party, but it was hard to tell for sure. In general they surely were not. But I think there was an attempt by people who were affiliated with the Communist Party to bring me in with them. It was easier to do that with me than with Frank because in the early years I did not have the political connections that he had. We were both active in politics, but his contacts were much stronger.

One person that I worked with in the community apparently was much more involved in the actual Communist Party than I re-

Chez Nous Club dance, ca. 1955. Peggy is second from right in back row; courtesy of the author.

alized. I was invited by this person's group, which opposed segregation in some way, to go to Washington to address the membership. Now, what membership, I wasn't sure. We were to leave early in the morning. Fortunately, Billy, our dog, got sick, and I didn't go. I found out later that this was a Communist front organization. It would have been a disaster if I had gone.

As time went on, I became more and more involved in Republican politics. There was a strong Republican tradition among black people in the South. Booker Washington, for instance, had been a leader in the Republican Party in Alabama. Frank was a Republican because his father in Ware Neck, Virginia, had been a Republican. In Virginia when Frank grew up, if black people weren't Republican, they just didn't get it. My father had been a Republican as well.

Frank became active in Republican circles in Lima and again in Poughkeepsie. Some white people on the board of the Bradfield Center in Lima were ultra-Republican. The one black person on the board was a Republican, too, and he talked about the value of having black people in every political party. Because of FDR and Mrs. Roosevelt, this was a time when many black people were switching their allegiance to the Democratic Party. I was again swimming against the tide.

I was not much interested in politics at first. I think that when I registered to vote in Poughkeepsie, it was as a Democrat. When I came to Syracuse, Frank wanted me to join him in the Republican Party. It didn't mean one thing or another at that time to me, I'll have to admit. I thought in local terms, and here the differences between the parties didn't seem too important. Both Frank and I felt, "Don't worry about what you call me, just get done what needs to get done."

The Republicans in Syracuse wanted—and got—black votes

from the Fifteenth Ward. The way they used to get these votes was to fold up a two dollar bill and put it in a matchbook, meet a guy on the street who was going to vote, and tell him, "Now so-and-so has done so much for you. When you go into the booth, this is what you do. And here are some matches for you." It was a bribe. A lot of people didn't want to carry two dollar bills because that was the payoff denomination.

Frank and Eugene Goldstein and Walter Welsh vowed to stop that matchbook thing. Gene Goldstein, who was black although his name didn't sound like it, was the top black person in the Republican Party locally. Father Walter Welsh, who was white, was the rector of Grace Episcopal Church at Madison Street and University Avenue, the scene of much civil rights activity in years to come. These three were united in trying to persuade the black community that voting meant something besides just pulling the lever for a candidate that somebody had told you to pull it for. They caught the dickens because many people were happy with things just the way they were.

The number of black people who actually took part in Republican Party activities was quite small. Frank and I worked at the polls for the Republicans, and we registered voters. Somehow the word got back to the state headquarters that there was a very strange person running around the streets of Syracuse—a black woman acknowledged to be a Republican. I met Governor Rockefeller, and before long I was appointed to every committee you can think of. If an organization needed someone who was black and Republican and a woman, it would call Gene Goldstein and Gene would call me. People seemed to think that I was the lone specimen in upstate New York who could spell!

In years to come, I would be appointed to the President's Committee on Health Education, which took me to the White

House. Also to the New York State Division of Criminal Justice Planning Board, where I was one of the black voices questioning the small number of paroles granted to black inmates. In 1976 I would be an alternate delegate to the Republican convention in Kansas City when Gerald Ford was nominated.

But to return to the late 1950s, I was still at the Salvation Army and not really happy with its outreach to the black community or lack thereof. About this time, Howard Gundy, dean of Syracuse University's School of Social Work, began to urge the Syracuse Health Department to hire its first social worker. Howard recommended me, and Dr. David Bigwood, commissioner of health, agreed to the idea. Dr. Bigwood said, "I don't know what she will do exactly, but it sounds to me like we do need her here."

In 1958, then, I became the director of public health-social work and kept this job until I retired in 1980. I moved into my office at the health department in the former Montgomery School on Montgomery Street. My welcome was not a very enthusiastic one, but I went through all of the sections of the health department and, in a very calm way, found out the problems related to getting health care to people.

In my new job, I would get a report of a suspicious situation in a neighborhood, often in the Fifteenth Ward. (Mailmen were one of our best sources of information.) Many times you could see from the street that something was the matter. Children coming out of an apartment looked like they hadn't eaten in a long while. Even the dogs and cats looked like they were starving. At the door, you would ask the children, "Where's your mother?" They would say, "She's in there," or "She's not out yet," pointing to a bedroom. Then you would know that prostitution was going on.

The police went with me to check on these situations. If nobody answered our knock, we would slide a piece of paper under the door, try to jostle the key loose, then pull the paper out, sometimes with a key actually on it, just like in the movies.

One of my duties at the health department was to run the social work program at Silverman Public Health Hospital on Renwick Avenue below Syracuse University. Silverman was our infectious disease hospital. Polio and tuberculosis patients went there. In the early 1960s, after the Sabin oral vaccine for polio came in, the health department put on a big push to vaccinate all of Syracuse using the sugar cube. I worked closely with the doctors at Silverman Hospital, but I also had to know the community in order to get it to cooperate. We got most of the people outside the inner city in to be vaccinated, notifying them by TV and trucks with loudspeakers. But the black community in the Fifteenth Ward would have no part of the program. "The Health Department's never done anything for us, so why should we get involved with this."

To combat this attitude, we went to the churches and their Sunday school classes, as well as to Dunbar Center and Huntington Family Center. We enlisted an army of little black children. It was the most beautiful thing you could imagine. They went house to house. We selected places where we could have clinics. We got tables and chairs from people in the neighborhood and set them up so that we could bring our nurses in.

It was really a children's crusade. People commented, "How in the world did you get those children out like that?" I said, "Churches are filled with these little kids every Sunday, going down the aisles, taking up money, ushering." The ministers rode in trucks and called out to everybody over loudspeakers. When we finished, we had vaccinated more than 90 percent of the black community.

We had people at Silverman Hospital who had contracted

polio. Two of them were black children. That also helped us get the black community motivated. Until this polio drive, there was a tendency in the medical community to write off the Fifteenth Ward. But nobody had seriously tried to work with that community. It took a lot of doing, but it also took a knowledge of the people who lived there. What do they know about the whole business? They knew about TB because there had been an outbreak of TB in the black community, but they didn't know as much about polio. Their participation in the vaccination drive was a turning point in the Fifteenth Ward, not so well known as later developments, but important.

Alcoholism, like communicable disease, was a big problem. In 1959 I joined with Ben Shove, the lawyer who was always involved in improving Syracuse, the Reverend William McConaghy of First Presbyterian Church on West Genesee Street, Della Black, Maria Farr, and others to found the Syracuse Brick House on Green Street. This was, and is, a wonderful alcoholism rehabilitation facility. I wanted it to serve both men and women. That didn't work out in the beginning, but later it did. We bought the house next door to the original Brick House for use by women, many of whom had been clients of mine when I was at the Salvation Army.

Peggy Wood and Chez Nous

Harriet Fields, Syracuse schoolteacher, now deceased

I was born in Lexington, Kentucky, and received a bachelor of science degree from Kentucky State University. My husband Holloway graduated from the University of Kentucky in 1951, becoming the first black person to graduate from an accredited engineering school below

*the Mason-Dixon line. After he was hired by General Electric in
Syracuse, New York, he returned to Kentucky and married me. I came to
Syracuse with him, earning a masters of science degree from Syracuse
University and becoming a math teacher in the Syracuse City School
District. It was then that I first met Peggy Wood, an extremely
successful woman who succeeded in endeavors that many of her
contemporaries did not dare to attempt.*

*Before I arrived in Syracuse, Peggy Wood, Evelyn Washington, and
Rena Hawkins had met to find ways to fill a void in services for black
citizens, particularly black women. They had invited others with similar
standards and goals to meet with them, organizing this group under the
name Chez Nous.*

*Chez Nous, meaning "at our house," met on a regular basis in the
homes of members. It elected officers and followed standard
parliamentary procedures as its members planned ways of improving
community life, especially for its young black people. It had another
important function, too: it gave its members the opportunity for social
relaxation and sharing—sharing ideas and beautifully prepared food, as
well as a common goal.*

*I first experienced Chez Nous when I was invited to a party at the
home of Charles (Chuck) and Ann Willie. Ann was a member of Chez
Nous, and Chuck was a faculty member at Syracuse University. At the
Willie home, a tall, attractive woman answered the door. This was Peggy
Wood. She greeted me warmly and graciously took me around the room,
making introductions and giving me, a young newcomer to the
community, a feeling of belonging. This was the beginning of a
friendship that we have maintained through the years. In time I became
a member of Chez Nous.*

*Peggy was a diligent worker in the organization. She identified
areas of need in the city, and Chez Nous responded to them. As a*

professional social worker with a very responsible administrative position at the Salvation Army, Peggy really knew the community. Her observations and suggestions were well received.

One of our service projects was the annual debutante ball. The proportion of black students in Syracuse that achieved high school graduation was abysmally low at that time. Our idea was to encourage graduates and show our pride in them by honoring them with a celebration. A suitable ballroom had to be rented. However, in those years there were none available for black citizens. To rent a ballroom, Chez Nous had to petition, negotiate, and appeal—sometimes to higher authority, and on one occasion all the way to New York's attorney general, when we were denied the use of a facility on the grounds of race. As a result of Chez Nous's efforts, several places became available not only to the club but to other black organizations as well.

In order to select debutantes, the club contacted guidance counselors, teachers, and principals, seeking candidates based on character recommendations, grades, student activities, and the like. The families of the selected girls were visited and informed of the honor. After this was done, Chez Nous held "charm school" classes, which included advice and practice in socially and morally acceptable behavior, in what to expect and how to prepare for college, and in proper attire for various occasions. This was followed by a "dry run" for the ball, when the girls practiced dancing and curtsying and, with their escorts, the proper walk.

We also gave advice on how to deal with the obstacles black women experienced in daily life, which were many. There were places that they weren't allowed to frequent. We would tell our young women how to deal with that refusal, making it a positive thing rather than have them feel, "Well, I'm defeated, and I'm not going to try."

On the night of the event, there was live music for ballroom dancing. No hip-hopping! (Peggy and Frank Wood themselves were good dancers and loved to waltz.) There was a receiving line of the girls and their escorts and parents. Each debutante and escort would be formally introduced, and there would be a grand march of the whole crowd of well over one hundred people—one time this was held in the War Memorial, a huge building downtown.

At Chez Nous meetings, we discussed other projects that we might undertake. We helped black college girls attending Syracuse University who wanted to live off campus. We arranged discussions of political issues, bringing in guest speakers to talk on what was happening throughout the country, as well as locally, such as urban renewal.

Peggy was a leader in all these activities. I would say that in her career Peggy possessed all of the qualities that made her a strong and successful administrator. She was an inspiration and a role model for young black women and many others, because she was able to combine her life as a wife and as a mother of high-achieving children with her role as community leader.

✿

Urban Renewal and YMED

When Brick House was getting under way, Syracuse was entering the action stage of urban renewal, which would transform the city. Urban renewal—sometimes called "black removal"—would in short order alter the Fifteenth Ward beyond recognition. Urban renewal was happening all over the United States. Congress had allocated money to wipe out "ghettos." This had been studied in Syracuse since the early fifties. Now the bulldozers were about to roll in. At the same time, the Fifteenth Ward was being sliced down the middle by Route 81, another sign of the times, as the Interstate Highway System seemed to have a fondness for black neighborhoods.

In 1959 a twenty-member Syracuse Urban Renewal Council was appointed by Syracuse's Mayor Henninger. I was on the council, along with Dr. Charles Willie of Syracuse University's Department of Sociology and Anthropology. Frank and I had known Chuck Willie since his graduate student days at Syracuse when he was a part of a group of bright young black men that included Bob Johnson, who went on to found Black Entertainment Television. Chuck, whose family background was similar to mine, came from Texas and had graduated from Morehouse College in Atlanta, which I knew well. Chuck and I complemented each other. He had produced a socioeconomic study of Syracuse for his Ph.D. dissertation and had a great academic knowledge of the Fifteenth Ward. And I knew the *people* in the Fifteenth Ward. The two of us suffered together through the whole urban renewal crisis.

The Syracuse Urban Renewal Council set up a relocation committee to plan the moving of people out of the path of the urban renewal. Chuck and I were put on this committee. The chairman was Bill Chiles from county government. Bill was black, but lived way out in Nedrow and unfortunately didn't know very much about the problems of the Fifteenth Ward. The big question for the committee was what should we do with the people in the area where there would be demolitions? Where will they go? Unspoken was the question how can the city keep the blacks together in a community rather than all over Syracuse? In other words, how can we prevent all these downtrodden people from moving out into the rest of the city?

At first, urban renewal did not take on the destructive tone that it eventually did, I think maybe because of Pioneer Homes. This public housing project, one of the first of its type in the United States, had opened in 1940. It was viewed in a positive light by the black community, even though most of the buildings were all white. The folks who lived in the one or two buildings for blacks were active politically. And then you had Salt City Homes on East Fayette Street, which had opened in 1950 for veterans. This also was seen in a favorable light. And I do think the positive effect of the polio vaccination campaign planted the idea that government action might not be all bad for the black community.

I myself was on the fence. Parts of the Fifteenth Ward were unquestionably slums. People should not have been forced to live in such conditions. Somebody needed to do something about that, and the "do something" was to get rid of the dilapidated buildings. The chance of persuading absentee landlords to rehabilitate their properties was nil. But most white participants in the urban renewal process never pictured who came out of those slums. Some of the leaders in this community today grew up in the Fifteenth Ward. Wonderful people lived there. It was a bitter pill to see this whole community bulldozed away.

The urban renewal program could have been a terrible tragedy in Syracuse, but it was not. When the Relocation Committee began work, urban renewal had already attracted a large amount of newspaper coverage because of violence in other parts of the country. In some other cities, officials had said in this block, that block, and so far around, these houses come down tomorrow. Little advance warning was given to leaders of the community. Predictably, the people affected didn't take it lying down.

The Relocation Committee received the worst abuse because its recommendations touched the lives of the people in the Fifteenth Ward. Though the higher-ups didn't pay attention to us all the time, at least we spoke up and tried to prevent violence. We worked with the churches. We visited many families when a block was selected to be torn down.

I remember going into a woman's house. She had five children, and she was a single mother. Her husband was not with her, but we later learned that he was working on a job and supporting them in addition to welfare. This house was one of the ones that was dilapidated on the outside. It looked like it could fall in at any minute. So I decided to go in and make a visit. I went in. Inside it was beautiful. Handmade curtains, things that you knew came out of the Salvation Army store but had been mended or painted. Landlords let the exteriors go downhill, but the tenants often did wonders inside.

There was also an upright piano. The mother said, "Mrs. Wood, where do you think we are going to move?" And I gave her an idea of what streets had apartments. She said, "I have to tell you I don't care. I've worried about it long enough, and I don't care where we go. But I want you to do one favor for me and that is to put in my record that I will not move out of this house unless my piano goes with me." I stood there with the tears rolling down my cheeks, and I said, "I will make sure that your piano goes wherever you go." She had these five kids, and I think four of them were girls. She wanted them all to learn how to play the piano. I was able to get a decent place for her and her family and the piano.

The Relocation Committee took the census book and drew circles showing where the people would move from where they were currently located. The lowest-income families would, in all probability, move into the first half-mile away from the urban renewal area. What it meant was that black people would suddenly find themselves in houses formerly occupied by whites, who were fleeing for the suburbs. Everything was now pointing to resegregation. You were just starting another Fifteenth Ward a half mile away from the urban renewal displacement. As new housing projects were proposed to house the people who had been uprooted, Father Walter Welsh of Grace Church, Frank, and Gene Goldstein tried—without success—to get them sited in the outskirts of Syracuse in order to prevent resegregation from happening.

The main outflow from the Fifteenth Ward went south, particularly down South State Street below Castle and Kennedy. The big houses there were cut up into apartments. A large outflow also went east along Genesee and Fayette Streets, where, again, big houses—some owned by leaders in the black community—were subdivided. Less migration occurred to the west, with Geddes Street as the outer limit. To the north there was little movement, just enough to barely desegregate that side of town. Whites were now leaving Pioneer Homes, and some of the displaced people could move in there.

In 1962, the first buildings of the new Central Village housing project were completed on State Street between Burt and Castle, not far south of the Fifteenth Ward. This is just what Father Welsh and Frank and Gene Goldstein had tried to prevent. Ben Shove had offered land he owned in Camillus in hopes that the housing project would attract both whites and blacks from all over the county and be truly integrated. But, instead, we ended up with a project on the edge of the urban renewal area. Oh, they called Ben everything under the sun, and it was hurtful to him. Of course, I adored him. Ben said, "Open it up to the *whole* of Onondaga County, including everybody in the Fifteenth Ward." Well, that was a war because the powers that be didn't want blacks out in the suburbs. No, no. They didn't want the blacks out there, and the blacks, for their part, didn't want lots of dysfunctional families congregated in one spot.

Pioneer Homes was a well-constructed project. People vied to get in there, especially black people who for a long time only had two buildings on the Townsend Street side. (There were those people, blacks as well as whites, who felt that Pioneer was for the "nice people" in the community.) Central Village, by contrast, was poorly built. Large families moved into Central Village. Originally, you had a few whites, but they weren't there long. It soon developed into all-black housing for families with lots of children.

But starting back in 1959, before ground was even broken for Central Village, Chuck Willie and I would get together night after night in one of the bars near my old Salvation Army office to talk about who could go where when the demolition began. I didn't detect any animosity toward me at first. Everyone knew that urban renewal was the coming thing nationally. Opposition to it had not built up yet in Syracuse. In the initial stages, the black community was looking to make the best of the situation and saw some of the positive side of it. But they had to have some *help* to see the positive side!

When the demolition began, the attitude changed, and my position was not so easy. Now we had those who were just against urban renewal *period.* "We don't want them coming into our neighborhood and destroying a community that has been cohesive for so long. We don't want any part of it." For instance, "Don't mess with Ashworth Place. Leave that alone." Most of the people on that street owned their own homes and planned to stay there. And the same was true on parts of Fayette Street. So I think people in the Fifteenth Ward began to see me in two lights, as someone who was trying to make the urban renewal disrupt people's lives as little as possible, but also as someone serving on the committees that made the whole thing happen. Of course, the clearing of the Fifteenth Ward and the construction of ill-conceived high-rise buildings was a done deal, whether I was on any committees or not.

The tension over urban renewal mixed with tension over desegregation of the public school system that led to the closing of predominantly black Washington Irving and Madison Schools in 1965. All of this was reflected in my church, which was an unusual church. But some background first. When Frank and I moved to Syracuse in 1950, my children and I joined Danforth Congregational Church, a white church on South Salina Street in what was then a white neighborhood. Danforth would close in 1969 after Route 81 cut it off from many of its congregants and as the community around it changed from white to black.

In 1950 Frank joined St. Philip's Church, an all-black Episcopal mission church on Almond Street at Washington Street. The attractive stucco building accommodated about three hundred parishioners if all the pews were full. Frank thought that St. Philip's was the most active black church in the community on social issues so he was willing to leave the Baptist church. Many leaders in the black community belonged there. They were people who sat on boards and who could be counted to participate in the push for civil rights. But even though these people for the most part had good jobs and good cars, their church was not self-supporting. In 1957 the Episcopal diocese closed it.

When St. Philip's folded, some people stopped going to church altogether, but many transferred to other Episcopal churches. By far the most went to Grace Church, whose rector was Walter Welsh, a leader in the civil rights movement locally. Frank and Walter were close friends, as I have already mentioned, and Frank naturally went to Grace, too. Grace had been integrated on far more than a token basis before St. Philip's closed. But with the arrival of people from St. Philip's—and a modest dropout of white parishioners—Grace became at least one-third black, moving in the direction of fifty-fifty. It became—and remains, I believe—unique in Syracuse in this respect.

Frank never pushed, but when things really got moving on civil rights in Syracuse, he thought I should come with him to Grace Church, which I did. But by now I was on the Relocation Committee of the Urban Renewal Council. How could I go to church and face the congregation when I was involved in moving people out of their homes?

Those were difficult times all around. One white friend of mine, an official with the city school district who had worked very well with me in the past, was a leading member of Grace Church. I sat in a pew near him. Grace was at the center of the demonstrations of the early sixties. After a while, my friend said, "I have worked all of these years in this community for good race relations, for services for black people, and I've given my life to it. But I'm not going to give another Sunday. I just can't take it. I'm leaving." And he did. Frank couldn't believe he had heard that, but I could. I understood it. This friend had labored long and hard against discrimination, but on Sunday he needed a respite.

When urban renewal was hitting Syracuse's black community, the civil rights movement nationally was coming to its peak. In 1960 the Greensboro, North Carolina, sit-ins commenced; in 1961 the Freedom Rides began; in 1962 James Meredith enrolled at the University of Mississippi; in 1963 Martin Luther King, Jr., mounted a campaign against segregation in Birmingham, Alabama, and delivered his "I Have a Dream" speech to the March on Washington; in 1964 Medgar Evers was assassinated in Jackson, Mississippi; and in 1965 the marches from Selma to Montgomery, Alabama, took place—to name only a few milestones. The national and the local were coming together. Urban renewal was the oil on the civil rights fire. Here was something you could see. The demolishing of the houses in the neighborhood affected the people directly.

In 1962 the Congress of Racial Equality or CORE campaigned against Syracuse's segregated schools. In 1963 it led picketing against urban renewal in which protesters climbed upon construction equipment and chained themselves to trucks. CORE and the NAACP held rallies at Grace Church. One Sunday during all of this, someone phoned in a bomb threat when services were in progress. Father Welsh told the congregation about the threat. The

Sunday school of about ninety children was evacuated to the sidewalk down Madison Street. After two or three people left, Walter Welsh delivered his sermon as usual—and no explosion occurred.

The protests in the streets were good because they called attention to what was going on. But they grew more out of Syracuse University than the Fifteenth Ward. Also the CORE-led picketing was short on answers to inner-city problems. I don't think that the black community here wanted to be led by CORE. The churches, the community centers, and the politicians had more effect in bringing about change and limiting violence than CORE, although it was CORE that got in the newspapers.

While picketing was going on at construction sites in 1963, another development was taking place. The prior year my friend Bill Walsh had been sworn in as mayor of Syracuse. Now he appointed a new Mayor's Commission on Human Rights. Mayor Walsh made Dean Ralph Kharas of Syracuse University's College of Law acting chairman. Before long Dean Kharas was replaced by Rabbi Irwin Hyman as chairman, and I was then made vice chairman. Bill Walsh said, "Peggy, I would like for you to be the chairman, but I think it would be better to let Rabbi Hyman do it and you be his assistant because you are a government employee and he's out in the community. He can do a lot of things that you probably can't do." The original commission of sixteen citizens was enlarged to twenty-six in 1965 when the scope of the organization was expanded to take in Onondaga County. The membership included the Right Reverend Ned Cole, Episcopal bishop of central New York, and Gerry Dietz of the Dietz lantern company. The commission was charged to identify discriminatory practices in the community and to seek to eliminate them.

When I joined the Commission on Human Rights, Frank said,

"Peggy, I can't think how much trouble you are going to get into!" He was right. In the beginning, the commission did not have an executive director. Rabbi Hyman was very active, but it so happened that he went on a long trip away from Syracuse in 1965, leaving me in charge. During his absence, a doctor from the Upstate Medical Center, Dr. Robert Hays, called to have a conference with me. Dr. Hays came to talk about what governmental agencies were doing to pregnant black teenagers in Syracuse.

Now I was sympathetic to what Dr. Hays was saying because I had seen how black people were sometimes treated. The health department when I got there had a clinic for pregnant school-age children. A certain well-connected doctor here in Syracuse was in charge. This doctor treated the girls like pariahs. He would call them ugly names to their faces. "Come in, you animals!" Terrible, awful. I could hear this going on from my office. The man would find opportunities to come in and sit at my desk and talk about how he felt about black people, which was horrible. He was Catholic. One of his stories was that he went to church one Sunday and there was an African Catholic to deliver the sermon, and how he felt about having such a person in *his* church. Well, my immediate goal was to get rid of this doctor, but that job was beyond me. Doctors close ranks to protect their own.

But, returning to Commission on Human Rights, Dr. Hays filed a formal complaint against at least the Health Department and the Syracuse City School District for discrimination against black pregnant adolescents. Bob Hays was a saint as far I was concerned for doing this. He was blowing the whistle on a terrible practice. When the school system suspected that a student was pregnant, certain things happened. Now this in theory applied to both white and black girls, but in practice overwhelmingly to black. White parents would usually find a way to send a pregnant daughter "on a trip," as I have mentioned, while black parents couldn't do that.

The school system would send a girl suspected of being pregnant to a physician at the police department to certify her condition. This formed the basis for expelling the girl from school and also enabled the school system to collect a certain per diem reimbursement from the state. That is what the school system was mainly looking for, the money. The girl had to go to the police department like a criminal. It was just a grand affair at the police department where they talked about the girls and the babies and what they were doing and what they said. They made fun of the girls. That's exactly what many in the police department wanted.

So the girl was humiliated and then expelled. Nobody made any attempt to find out why these teenage girls were becoming pregnant so young, and not very much attempt was made to give prenatal care to these girls. As a result, infant mortality in the Fifteenth Ward was sky high.

The reaction to Dr. Hays's complaint was explosive at the health department. Dr. Bigwood, the health commissioner, was furious. My standing at the health department went into steep decline. But Dr. Bigwood came around in time. Dr. Hays appeared at the Commission on Human Rights to talk about his charges, and, of course, everything he said made sense. These practices had to stop. As a result of the complaint, the health department and the school district took a new look at their whole program for pregnant adolescents—and something very good came out of this study.

Those of us who were in favor of providing medical services and education together began to write up what we wanted. I knew that the former Washington Irving School on Madison Street was scheduled to be torn down as a part of urban renewal. Sidney Johnson from the school district, Dr. John Hagen from Upstate, and I, along with others from the health department, went over to the building and staked out the rooms we wanted, our clinic, the whole thing. Now, nobody had said that's what we could have, but we wrote up our program and went over there and staked out two floors. On each room we put a sign up, just as if the thing were really going to happen.

Providing medical care on school property was absolutely against state regulations. There was no school district in the state where they had an active medical program going on in a school building. We had to rewrite the program so that it was described as an education program. We did secure Washington Irving School before the wrecking ball. As a result, we were the first school in the state that had medical care on the premises.

We called what we were setting up the Young Mothers Educational Development Program or YMED, which sounded educational but got the medical point across in the abbreviation. We planned to have classes from the sixth grade up, as well as a clinic with five or six beds and a nursery with twelve cribs and twelve rocking chairs for the mothers. We had already identified twelve pregnant girls, the youngest of whom was a twelve-year-old. We also had a room where we would have graduation exercises and places for their parents to sit. The plumbers and pipefitters union installed pipes in our clinic for us to hang sheets from as partitions. Stickley gave us furniture. Planned Parenthood sent us a social worker from New York City and paid her salary.

The YMED Program opened in the fall of 1965 but really began full operation in the late spring of 1966. Pregnant teenagers would come to YMED at just about the time they would otherwise have been expelled from school. They took their classes at YMED, which were taught by teachers from the Syracuse school district. The prospective mothers had prenatal care in the YMED clinic. When it came time to have the baby, they went to the old St. Mary's Hospital on Court Street where Dr. Hugh Clark delivered them. Then the mothers returned to YMED and resumed their classes with the baby in the nursery, receiving good postnatal care.

A mother could stay at YMED as long as her school permitted. Six months after delivery would not have been unusual. (During this time, we might also have had to find a home for the mother and baby because a number of parents turned their unwed pregnant daughters out on the street.) When the mother started back to her regular school, there was always a problem. The baby had been well taken care of in the YMED nursery. Where would the baby go now during the day? Usually we were able to persuade the mother's parents to take her back. In some rare situations, the mother and the baby's father got married. The police would always be after the girl to disclose the name of the father. In a way, that was good because a lot of these guys were no-good people, who hung around and preyed on these young girls.

The educational side of YMED was headed by Bob DiFlorio, later superintendent of schools for Syracuse. He was our principal. Dr. John Hagen was our medical director. Dr. Howard Osofsky and Dr. Bob Long were on the medical staff. All of them—and many others I'm not mentioning—made YMED happen. As did, over the years, Nick Pirro from the county legislature, who saw to our funding. The result was that, by the early 1980s, well over two thousand babies had been born with proper medical care, and hundreds of mothers had continued with their educations. It was just wonderful to see what could take place if you stuck by it—even in Syracuse with all its problems, if you stuck by it and got enough people to come with you.

When we were starting YMED, I called all the public schools to tell them about the program. To pass the word to the parochial schools, I called someone in the Catholic hierarchy locally. I asked him for some estimate of the number of Catholic teenagers who were pregnant. He said, "Peggy, you're asking me something that I couldn't *possibly* help you with, because we never have had a pregnant girl in the Catholic schools. I don't think we're going to have any now." But he said, "Had you asked me about girls who were forced to leave school because of mononucleosis or because of stomach ulcers, that would have been a different question." Now that is the way we kept our statistics in this county about infant birth and mortality!

The first twelve girls in YMED were all black and mostly, if not entirely, from the Fifteenth Ward. Oh, the stories that went around about these children being so bad. It was a shame. Somebody posted a sign saying that you could only enter Washington Irving School if you accepted condoms. The rumor mill claimed we had a big box on the outside of the building where anybody could pull a lever and condoms would fall out. It was whispered around that YMED was just adding lots of little black illegitimate children to the community.

But soon we began to be contacted for help by white people who didn't live in the Fifteenth Ward. They wanted their teenagers to come to Washington Irving School. We had a couple of pregnant girls who came to us that way. So we had to have school buses. We picked them up and we brought them to YMED. Quickly the ratio of black to white became about fifty-fifty, including mothers from all over Onondaga County.

Most of our YMED students returned to their prior schools and graduated, if they graduated, at these schools. But some mothers were seniors when they came to us and could not return to their old schools in time for graduation. For these girls, we had special graduation exercises at YMED complete with printed programs and outside speakers. In 1968 Bernice Wright, dean of Syracuse University's College of Home Economics, would deliver the commencement address to YMED graduates whose regular schools were Central, Corcoran, Nottingham, and Fulton. Almost all the girls' parents came to these exercises. They came with their cameras and these poor little things walking across with their stomachs way out . . . It was beautiful.

The Commission on Human Rights led to YMED and the benefit to the community that I have described. Mayor Walsh's decision to establish the commission was vindicated. But the commission worked in other areas as well. To give one example, it took up the question of employment opportunities for black people in Syracuse, particularly with the power company, Niagara Mohawk. Employers would not promote blacks above entry-level positions. (I saw this firsthand: an executive at Crucible Steel, whom I knew at Danforth Congregational Church, could only get my son a menial summer job when he was at Bucknell and an A student in engineering.) The young black people here who graduated from high school ended up working in the basement of places like Crucible. You can't do a thing about being black. If you're black, you're black. I don't care how much education you get, I don't care how much traveling you do, how much money you have, you can never get away from the fact that you're black. And if you were black in the mid-1960s and there was somebody else who was not black, then the somebody else would get the position.

Employers began to understand that they had to open up job promotion to black people. At the same time, retail merchants began to understand that they needed to make their stores welcoming places for blacks. I had a hand in this.

I always felt so much a part of downtown. I loved it. I went there all the time. One particular store downtown was the Singer sewing machine shop on Salina Street. I noticed that every time I went to the shop there was a nondescript person who followed me around. So finally I said, "Why are you following me?" He said, "Because they told me that you might steal something." So I said, "Well, what's in here that you think I would steal? I can't carry any of these machines out." And he said, "Well, you know, we don't cater to niggers."

I thought about having received a Singer sewing machine on my sixteenth birthday from my mother and how much I loved that machine. Then to have gone in this shop . . . I decided to walk Salina Street and see how many of the stores had in their windows anything that would indicate that black people were welcome. I started this campaign by myself of walking the streets downtown to see how much of the material in the store windows in any way related to the needs of the black people.

One day I walked along Warren Street where there was an S. S. Kresge Company dime store. A little black girl was looking in the window at a black doll. It was very rare that anything related to blacks was placed in store windows, but there was this one doll. The little girl didn't know that I was watching her. This little girl's face was beaming. I stood there with the tears just rolling down my cheeks. I thought, "Now nobody can tell me that they have *any* reason for not having that kind of a display in the window." After that I noticed that Chappell's department store had no black mannequins. So then I began a crusade. Chappell's and other department stores said they could paint some of their white mannequins black and put them in the window. I said, "No. The thing should represent a real black person or at least be so dark that black people will know it represents them."

None of the department stores—Witherills, Deys, Chappell's had any idea how to do this. So the merchants got together and paid my way to New York to visit the mannequin factory. I went up and down Seventh Avenue. The most common black mannequin was modeled after Diahann Carroll. After I located a source for black mannequins, Syracuse stores bought them—the ones like Diahann Carroll, as well as mannequins of black males and children. It was like at the end of the war. Black people began to walk up and down Salina Street and see mannequins that looked like them. Some downtown stores still shadowed black people because they thought blacks would be stealing. But if a store added black mannequins, that would at least give store employees a feeling that black people were welcome, and it did make a big difference.

A Syracuse Friendship

Charles V. Willie, Charles W. Eliot Professor of Education
    Emeritus, Harvard University

I first met Peggy and Frank Wood in 1950 when they moved to Syracuse, New York, because Frank had been invited to be the director of the Dunbar Center, a settlement house serving a largely black population in the inner city. Frank came first; later that year, his family joined him. While alone in Syracuse, Frank found temporary housing at the Alpha Phi Alpha fraternity at Syracuse University, the first fraternity house on campus occupied by blacks. I had been initiated into this fraternity at Morehouse College in the 1940s while studying for a bachelor's degree. In 1949, I had enrolled in Syracuse University to study for a doctorate of philosophy in sociology.

With both of us living in the Alpha house, Frank and I soon became friends. We had much common ground. For one thing, we had both attended Atlanta University for our first level of postgraduate studies. Frank and Peggy had matriculated at Atlanta University for graduate study in social work; I earned a master's degree from the same school in sociology. This friendship with Frank Wood extended to his family when they arrived in Syracuse. I "house-sat" for the Wood family when they were on vacation.

At the time that Peggy and Frank Wood moved to Syracuse, E. Franklin Frazier, a famous black sociologist at Howard University, estimated that only one-eighth of black families in the United States were able to maintain a middle-class way of life. Today, according to my research, one-fourth to one-third of black families can be classified as middle class.

Two unique characteristics of middle-class black families are (1) joint participation in the labor force by husband and wife, and (2) the redistribution of decision-making power within the family between husband, wife, and children. Peggy and Frank Wood were among the starters of this national socioeconomic movement toward middle-class status among black families.

One could say Peggy and Frank Wood were perfect manifestations of these new practices a half century ago. Even though they had children, both husband and wife were employed initially in nonprofit social service agencies—she as a social worker with the Salvation Army and he as executive director of the Dunbar Center. Later in their careers, both Peggy and Frank accepted appointments as public administrators in local government—she as director of social work in the Department of Public Health and he as director of research of Onondaga County, New York.

The two-career family movement affected all population groups but was led by black, middle-class women like Peggy Wood. A chapter by Joe Feagin, "Black Women in the American Work Force," in The Family Life of Black People, *a book I edited in 1970, reported that "the traditional role of the American women . . . is changing in the direction of wife and worker." Feagin argued that "black . . . women pioneered these combined role-sets long before large proportions of white women began to enter the workforce."*

The two-career family like that of Peggy and Frank Wood has led to a new egalitarian model regarding the distribution of decision-making power within the family. Black middle-class families like the Woods were pioneers in establishing this new democratic arrangement. I have discovered in my research, published as A New Look at Black Families, *that "white families are increasingly fashioning their families in the egalitarian model first developed by middle-class, black families." Sociologist Bart Landry, author of* Black Working Wives, *also sees the contemporary black middle class as providing leadership for a new family paradigm.*

The contribution of families like Peggy and Frank Wood's to this new egalitarian family form in America—a form that supports the creative participation of wives in work outside the home as professionals, as well as jointly with their husbands rearing their children—was most valuable. It frequently is omitted or its origin forgotten in the chronicles of our recent history and contemporary way of life.

Peggy and I had a profound interest in community affairs. We both served on an Urban Renewal Advisory Committee, concerned with the relocation of individuals affected by urban renewal. We also had a shared interest in public health—I, as an instructor of preventive medicine at the State University of New York Upstate Medical Center, and she as director of social work in the Department of Public Health. Our collaboration continued when I later served as assistant professor, associate professor, and finally full professor at Syracuse University, until my appointment at Harvard University in 1974. We had personal contacts, too; our families were both members of Grace Episcopal Church in Syracuse.

Peggy was extraordinary as a low-profile negotiator on behalf of the black community. I remember one incident when she and I took on a powerful real estate agent in the city who wanted his company to participate in the federally sponsored urban renewal program in Syracuse. We demanded a no-discrimination pledge in exchange, and he complied. The City Planning Commission supported our effort. In the process of resisting housing discrimination, we had to cultivate a common interest with the City Planning Commission, which held the legal authority. This we did, using the empathetic and community organization skills that Peggy and I derived from our graduate studies in social work and sociology.

Of the many good interventions that Peggy sponsored, one most dear to her and most valuable to the community was the Young Mothers Educational Development Program (also known as the YMED Program). It was Peggy's strong belief that premature and unwanted pregnancies should not be a barrier to the educational progress of females who wanted to complete secondary schooling. Through hard work and perseverance, she persuaded the public school policy makers and others who were uncomfortable in dealing with this matter to do the right thing.

Of her many accomplishments, the YMED Program was probably one of the greatest. Peggy knew that, as the slogan of the United Negro College Fund puts it, "a mind is a terrible thing to waste," and she would neither rest nor relax until the community gave to its pregnant young people the privilege of another chance to complete their high school education. This was a delicate matter for which to mobilize community-wide support. Nevertheless, Peggy did it. She helped the Syracuse metropolitan community live up to its collective responsibility of rescuing the perishing and caring for the fallen.

The Origins of the Young Mothers Educational Development Program

Robert C. Hays, medical doctor, now deceased

I grew up in York, Pennsylvania, served in the Army in World War II, and received my undergraduate degree from Johns Hopkins University. After Johns Hopkins Medical School and postdoctoral training in obstetrics and gynecology, I came to Syracuse in 1961. Here I was primarily affiliated with Syracuse Memorial Hospital, now Crouse Memorial Hospital, as well as a full-time faculty member at Upstate Medical Center.

I was the director of the clinic at Crouse Hospital when I noted a curious thing. Some chap, whom I later found out was the school physician for Syracuse, was going around and flagging the nurses and writing down names. When I inquired what he was doing, I was told, "Oh yes, he's the school doctor. He comes around, and we're instructed to give him the names of any of the school girls who've become pregnant." Horrified by this violation of the nurse-patient and doctor-patient relationship, I put a stop to it at once. Then this doctor stopped by my office for what turned out to be a rather confrontational, unpleasant visit.

The school physician had come to scold me for impeding progress. He explained that the reason he was taking names was to conserve some of the state budget payments to Syracuse. If a girl was absent, there was no reimbursement, but if she had been excused for medical reasons, such as pregnancy, the reimbursement came through.

He explained that when he identified a pregnant school girl, he instantly terminated her education, even if she was only one or two weeks away from graduation. There was one particular case I came across where the girl was on the honor roll, an excellent student with many voluntary activities, who was highly thought of by her classmates. She was literally kicked out of school mere weeks before graduation and was not allowed to attend the ceremony because she was pregnant. This was an era when the attitude toward pregnancy was a great deal different than it is now. At that time, even a married, pregnant teacher who was "showing" would be interrogated by her supervisor and dismissed, allegedly to avoid scandal and disruption in the classroom.

"You will cease and desist from making things difficult for me," the school physician demanded. "You will cooperate and together we'll keep the school system funded." I informed this doctor that there was no way I would conform to his request. I saw his strategy as dreadfully unfair and in violation of the civil rights of these kids—black or not black. I also saw it as medically unsound. Since the word was out as to what happened when a pregnancy was diagnosed, these kids would do anything to avoid discovery. The policy encouraged them to avoid prenatal care until a very late date, often until they were in labor. As a result, the quality of their obstetric care was very poor indeed.

I devised a plan. Since the great majority of these girls were black or, as we said back in those days, "colored," I decided to write a letter of formal complaint to the mayor's own Commission on Human Rights and have the commission evaluate this problem. To be honest, my views at that time were quite liberal—left of liberal. I cited discrimination against young black girls as a way of crushing this Draconian school district stance of kicking the kids out of school. I hoped to negotiate an improved, modernized way of handling these kids, offering them health care and coming up with a more innovative education effort.

When the Commission on Human Rights called me in for a formal discussion of my complaint, I met, for the first time, Mrs. Frank Wood. Peggy smiled. In fact, she looked rather serene throughout the whole meeting, while the others, including Dr. Franklyn Barry, superintendent of schools, and Dr. David Bigwood, commissioner of health, looked unhappy or hostile. We talked afterward, and she was very encouraging. I remember that, at one point, there was a show of hands, and the only person who held up her hand and voted with me was Peggy Wood.

I proposed providing the girls education and medical care, but also child care at the school. Peggy thought that was a wonderful *concept, but most people in attendance seemed stunned at the very idea. This began my social, political, and, you might say, moral bonding with Peggy Wood.*

I found out later that Mayor Walsh had caught wind of this problem and had called Dr. Bigwood and Dr. Barry. The mayor's directive was simply: "Solve it!" With this impetus from Mayor Walsh, discussions followed that led to the founding of the Young Mothers Educational Development Program, or YMED, which opened in the school year 1965–66. This program had the participation of the Health Department, the school system, and the Department of OB/GYN at the College of Medicine, chaired by Dr. Robert E. L. Nesbitt Jr. The earliest workers in the YMED clinic were Dr. Howie Osofsky and Dr. John Hagen. A number of social workers and psychologists were assigned, and a comprehensive program was set up.

I later found that the Health Department and the city school district

collaborated in an effort to get me fired from Upstate, but the attempt
failed. At that time I was untenured, and Upstate's president could have
gotten rid of me, but he stood his ground. A very uncomfortable
Professor Nesbitt suggested a number of times that maybe I could be a
little bit more discreet, a little bit more politic, check with him before
filing official complaints, etc., etc. After I had pursued some of the
rumors and learned that efforts were being made to unseat me, I thought
at least one letter of support might be useful in my personnel file. Peggy
wrote a letter to the president of Upstate, asserting that my efforts, from
her vantage point, were constructive and progressive. So there was at
least one letter that wasn't negative in my folder.

Peggy Wood and the YMED Program

John H. Hagen, medical doctor, retired

I was born and raised in Buffalo, New York, and attended the University
of Buffalo. After that, I went to Upstate Medical Center in Syracuse,
followed by a residency in OB/GYN at Upstate.

In 1965 the YMED program sprang out of nowhere in the
Washington Irving School. At first the program was very confusing.
The only person who knew what she was doing was Peggy Wood. She
was an excellent social worker, concentrating on health problems. She
was worried about how poorly teenagers were doing with their
pregnancies; their own health was often uncertain, and in too many
cases their babies did not survive. Peggy had clear ideas about how to
change this, and of the elements that ended up in YMED, 98 percent
were Peggy Wood's suggestions.

Other programs had the experience that if you refer students out of
school to go to a doctor's appointment, you let them out the door and

only a quarter of them would make it there and who knows if they'd ever come back. Peggy's whole idea was, to make this work, all services had to be in one building. Then we could go back and forth from room to room rather than chasing all over the world. So she organized the medical clinics and got the two pediatricians, Dr. Robert Austin and Dr. Robert Long, to take turns working, along with Dr. Howard Osofsky and me in obstetrics. Bob DiFlorio was the first principal of our school, assigned by the school district to handle the educational part.

We had an OB clinic in the school building, which wasn't legal. We had a pediatric clinic for the newborn babies, and that wasn't legal for a school. And we ended up having a nursery in the school, and that wasn't legal either.

If I had tried to do this, I would have been turned down flat. But Peggy had been around a long time and knew everybody. I think people were a little scared of her because she had so much political influence, not only in the Health Department, but in Albany—even with the governor. "Maybe we shouldn't go out of our way to oppose her"—that was the attitude. I was impressed with how easily she would organize things that hadn't been done before as if we'd been doing them all along.

The community accused us of opening a country club to encourage teenage pregnancy. The YMED program also wasn't popular because at first it served mainly poor black girls. The general feeling up to the mid-1960s was "If girls are pregnant, they ought to go out of town. Conceal the baby and give it up for adoption, and don't come back here until you're not pregnant anymore." This worked with some of the middle-class kids, but not with the inner-city black kids. They just hung in there. So, because they hung in, it looked like the only pregnant kids in the city were black.

The politics were "We're not going to spend any public money on that. That's immoral. They shouldn't have babies." It was always a fight.

But Peggy was able to get the county legislature every year to renew the budget, thanks primarily to Nick Pirro, who's currently county executive, but then was the head of the legislature's health committee. He personally fought on Peggy's side and kept YMED going over the years.

We didn't have any trouble finding patients. Heads of schools didn't want pregnant girls around. There was that general feeling that they knew something the other girls didn't. Also, pregnant girls are subject to mild medical problems that make everybody nervous as hell. So as soon as the authorities found out they had a pregnant girl, they would ship her to us. The YMED started out pretty much as an inner-city black program, but soon it became almost half and half county and city kids, and white and black. By then, it had really turned out good for everybody, because now you had a racial mix.

Peggy pointed out that from a public health point of view, confirmed by the obstetric literature, pregnant teenagers were, in the new phrase of the late 1960s, "at risk." There was a high death rate among teenage mothers and there was an even higher perinatal death rate, in that the baby didn't survive. Rates of premature labor and Caesarean sections were also high in teenagers. But we found at YMED that if mothers got good prenatal care and we recognized problems early and treated them, they were a very healthy group. In fact, the prematurity rate that we had in YMED was down almost to 6 percent, which was close to the national average. The perinatal mortality rate was zero in the first hundred we had at YMED. After the first five hundred, it was around one or two percent. It was amazing, the change.

I learned an awful lot from Peggy Wood personally. One day I said to Peggy, "Boy, these girls are tough. I've worked with a lot of these teenagers in Upstate clinics, and they don't want to listen to you too much. They don't like to be examined. They're really a tough group."

She said, "No, you're a tough doctor. Ever think of that?" I said I didn't think so! But she said, "Well, it's something that we all have to learn. You've got to find out why they don't want this and take time to talk with them and try to impress them with how good you are."

Peggy was a mentor to all of us. I always remember we had a young girl who was gaining too much weight, and we tried to put her on a diet. We gave her a diet sheet to follow every day. It wasn't working, and Peggy said, "Did you ever ask her whether she could read and write, Dr. Hagen?" I said, "No, we're in a school. I figured somebody would have told me that." Peggy said, "I'm telling you now." We had a student that couldn't read or write, and we were giving her literature to read!

Peggy organized things that I'd never believed I'd get into. As part of an effort to get the staff, including the doctors, to relate better socially with the students, Peggy arranged to have a monthly outing. We—staff, students, and their babies, if they had already delivered—started out by going to Thornden Park and cooking hot dogs. Peggy also thought that girls this age were supposed to be getting physical education. The Hutchings Psychiatric Center had a big swimming pool in one of its buildings. So she arranged for the students all to go there with the teachers to swim. She didn't get me to go to that!

Peggy and I encouraged each baby's father to come in with the girl to see the doctor, hoping that he'd get excited about more than just having intercourse: "Hey, that's my baby in there." We'd let him listen to the heartbeat. We almost had the whole hospital turn over when we invited the unwed fathers to come up and see their babies born. But after we argued with the hospital, they let us do it.

I was really excited about that and so was Peggy. The father, we hoped, was going to bond with the baby and take better care of the mother, rather than dumping her. Didn't work on one person! They all dumped her, every one of them. We didn't get one person that that worked with! They all thought that it was sort of interesting to see a baby born. But they were like voyeurs: they showed up in the hospital and watched the baby being born and held it briefly and that was it.

Peggy and I used to argue with people about a term that just annoyed the hell out of us: recidivism. *That's a legal word usually applied to a criminal. People who wrote about teenage pregnancy said the "recidivism rate" was high. In other words, girls would get pregnant again, implying that this was a crime they were committing, putting it in the same ball game as robbery or rape. Peggy used to cringe when people used that term in meetings. She would carry on. There were some things that really got her upset.* Repeat pregnancy *is the term we used.*

A Summing Up

In 1964 my daughter Yvonne married a man from the Volta region of Ghana. Frank and I then began a series of trips to Africa to be with these two and our grandchildren. Later our son became managing director for Union Carbide in Nigeria, another reason for visits to Africa. I spent time, as well, in Trinidad and Tobago as a participant in a cultural exchange program called Partners of the Americas. I helped the people there start vegetable gardens and small businesses. In 1980 Frank and I retired, which gave us more opportunity to roam the world.

They say that traveling broadens you. It also lets you see your own experience a little more clearly. And I have had a lot of it to look back on. William Howard Taft was in the White House when I was born. In some small way, I have been a part of a thrilling story—the coming into their own of black people as full citizens in this country.

When I was born down in Tallahassee, total segregation was the rule. *Nothing* was integrated. You went to the train station, for example, hot and thirsty. There would be a white spigot over here and a black one over there. Half the time the white spigot worked and the black one didn't, which meant you didn't drink. You never even thought to go over to the white spigot. Now, more than ninety years later, we have a black woman as secretary of state.

My story here has been a local one, about what I have seen in the places I have lived. But I would like to end with a reminiscence of something that touched me from a distance, a recollection of Martin Luther King, Jr.

On Auburn Avenue in Atlanta, Martin Luther King was known as a big guy. He went off to Crozier Seminary in Pennsylvania after he finished at Morehouse. My husband Frank's brother Marcus was a classmate of Martin Luther King's at Crozier. Marcus did not like him. Marcus thought he was too slow to stand up for the black poor. To Marcus, if you were a black minister, you were supposed to be *loud* when you preached to your flock, and he didn't see that King had this in him. He had not in any way exhibited the kind of person that he would become later. He had not had time to do that. He wasn't *it* when he started.

While the Montgomery bus boycott was going on, and other events in the South leading up to the drive to desegregate Birmingham in 1963, I was far away in the North. Martin Luther King was the leader down there, but not so much up here. He was not yet the towering figure he would soon become—not for me and not for most of black Syracuse. Then in August 1963 came the March on Washington and the "I Have a Dream" speech.

At first it was not easy to fill buses to go to Washington, but in the end we had four. I remember how difficult it was to get any excitement in our black community about going down to hear his speech, as remarkable as that seems now. Frank and I got on the bus around midnight and we arrived in Washington early in the morning. The people were all out, and they were blowing horns, and they were waving as this great stream of buses came down every highway. It was something that I had never participated in, and it was wonderful.

This young man Martin Luther King got up there and

preached to us, and you knew every word came from the heart. Now he had it. He had gotten it. He had *inhaled* it, you see! And now Syracuse knew, as did the people in the South, that this was our man. This person had become a Booker T. Washington or Du Bois, and with a voice that would be heard around the world.

Black people here in Syracuse saw what could happen if they were united. There would be no more accepting the two dollar bills to vote for a candidate. Black people were becoming comfortable with having their own opinions and not just reacting to somebody else. The number of people in Syracuse's black community was expanding rapidly. More people assumed leadership roles and were not afraid of losing their jobs if they spoke up. Partly because of urban renewal, blacks were no longer encased in one little shell. Most moved near the Fifteenth Ward, it is true, but pockets now began to spring up all over the city. Blacks were beginning to buy homes and to move their children into different neighborhoods. Through YMED and in other ways, their health care was improving, and job opportunities were opening up above the entry level.

What a joy it has been to take part in all of this—to leave things better than I found them!

Afterword

As mentioned in the preface, this book began as an oral history interview of Peggy Wood. How well I remember my first taping session with her. Peggy seated herself nervously in her favorite rocking chair. I placed the cassette tape recorder by the rocker on a little table. Despite my would-be calming demeanor, Peggy eyed the recorder apprehensively. Then, with her permission, I pushed the "on" button and began asking questions. Peggy began answering the questions—and rocking across the rug away from that tape machine. Peggy would rock, and I would move the little table across the floor to keep it near her. Only when we reached the other side of the room did the interviewing enter more placid waters.

That was July 12, 2001. Over the course of the next eight months, I returned often to Peggy Wood's home on Nursery Lane in Comstock Commons for further taping. Before long—apprehension completely dispelled—Peggy would ask, "Is it on?" to be sure that the machine was capturing what she had to say. Before long it also became apparent that my relationship to Peggy would be less that of an oral historian to subject and more that of a collaborator who would help her get her story down on the page. Accordingly, the two of us worked together toward that goal.

When the tapes were transcribed and edited, it seemed that

Peggy and Frank Wood, ca. 1960; courtesy of the author.

the main story was the emergence of black people into full citizenship and Peggy's role in that, both as participant and exemplar. That story has a natural conclusion in the late 1960s. Not that the years thereafter were uneventful.

In the 1960s, Peggy and Frank Wood's son, Frank III, married and started his career as an executive with Union Carbide Corporation, a career that would take him to Nigeria, Pakistan, and other countries. Their daughter, Yvonne, married a lawyer from Ghana and took advanced degrees in social work and psychology, teaching in both Ghana and New York. (Over time Peggy became grandmother to five grandchildren, all of whom are now grown.) Her husband Frank left the Dunbar Center to become the director of research and public information for Onondaga County, the first black division head in the history of the county.

In the 1970s, Peggy continued as director of public health-social work while accepting numerous other responsibilities, such as her appointment to the New York State Division of Criminal Justice Planning Board. She also took a leading role in what was called "Partners of the Americas," a cooperative venture between Central New York and Trinidad and Tobago. She and Frank began traveling to Africa to visit their children, particularly after Frank's retirement in 1979 from county government and Peggy's retirement in 1980 from the health department. In 1991 Frank died.

Today Peggy, while of limited mobility, is as engaged in life as ever. At age ninety-three, her impatience with injustice remains unabated.

—P. B.